MW01641394

Invoking Intercessory Prayer Power

Mediating Modern-day Miracles

George K. Chacko, Ph.D.

Daystar Communications
P.O. Box 613
Cary, North Carolina 27512-0613

ISBN: 0-9643812-3-0

First printing March 1997

Printed in the U.S.A.

Scripture references used:
NIV – New International Version
KJV – King James Version
PHI – J.B. Phillips
NEB – New English Bible
MOF – Moffatt

Dedicated affectionately to
Our first grandson
Josiah Stephen Chacko
Second of the second generation of
American-born Chackos
Who, at age 4,
Perceives the power of personal prayer

Foreword

No discipline is more neglected and more necessary in our generation than the practice of prayer for, ultimately, this is the means by which a believer is drawn into the communion with God that is the heart of any authentic Christian relationship. Having been saved by grace, we are inheritors of all the benefits of children of the most High God. In prayer, we are introduced to the means of access to the Father. George Chacko has produced a guide to the way in which we are able to approach the Father, in words that please Him most. Neither in prayer nor in praise is there more delight in the heart of God than to receive again His own Word processed and prayed back. George has taken special delight both in learning and teaching people, over several continents, how this may most effectively be used. I would commend this volume as yet another tool by which Christians are drawn into the deepest of intimate experiences to share in the power and the privilege of learning what it is to be children adopted by the grace of God into the fellowship to which He calls us. I trust this book will be used by many for the deepening of their own spiritual lives to the glory of God and the enrichment of the Kingdom.

DR. ROBERT M. NORRIS
SENIOR PASTOR, FOURTH PRESBYTERIAN CHURCH
FEBRUARY 20, 1997

Preface

This is a **practical** book on prayer power. Prayer for our concrete needs is empowered when we invoke the Risen Lord's commitment: "I will do whatsoever you ask in my name." Using 40 instances of answered prayer in five different types of concrete needs (listed on pp. 139–140), we discuss the practice of prayer power. The prayer power testimony covers events from 1897 B.C. to 1997 A.D. It spans the Old and New Testaments, and in our times, four churches in the United States and Asia.

Part I: Resurrection Power in Intercessory Prayer discusses how our invocation goes far beyond common sense (Ch. 1,2), and how the Lord provides resources to meet concrete needs in the instantaneous timeframe (exact time) and in the future timeframe (expectant time) (Ch. 3). Answered concrete needs are miracles: events which have about 1 chance in 1 billion (Ch. 4). When the Lord asks us to transmit His message on the future occurrence of these miracles, we affirm His Resurrection Power: the transcending of dimensions–from the finite to the infinite (Ch. 5).

The answered concrete needs comprise five types: financial, physical, professional, relational, and spiritual.

We witness: "There was a need; the Lord met it." But those facing similar situations want to know: How did He meet it? Especially if the answer came in engineering time (displaced future)?

Part II: Exact, Expectant, and Engineering Time in Answered Intercession discusses different types of concrete needs by resources and timeframes.

(1) *Recompensing Resources* at exact time are required for professional needs in Ch. 6; and for relational, financial, physical, and spiritual needs in Ch. 7.

(2) *Renewing Resources in Expectant Time* are required for physical, professional, and relational needs in Ch. 8; and for financial, physical and professional needs in Ch.9.

(3) *Renewing Resources in Engineering Time* are required for professional, spiritual, and financial needs in Ch. 11.

Part III: Practicing Prayer Power discusses six steps, from discerning what to pray for to offering thanks to the Lord for identified answers. It uses two acronyms DISCO (Chs. 12-14), and LISCO (Chs. 15-17). We do not rush in where we see a need, but await the guidance of the Spirit to discern the demand, claim a promise, and access our own resources (DISCO). We listen to the Lord, communicating the message He gives us, and offer thanks for His provisions (LISCO).

May you be empowered to access the power that is yours though prayer!

GEORGE K. CHACKO

Contents

Part I: Resurrection Power in Intercessory Prayer

1. Practicing Prayer Power 1

2. Claiming the Lord's Commitment 10

3. God's Provisioning in Exact Time and Expectant Time 23

4. Measures of Miracles-Ancient and Modern 30

5. Reality of Resurrection in Prayer Power 37

Part II: Exact, Expectant, and Engineering Time in Answered Intercession

6. Recompensing Resources for Exact Time-I 50

7. Recompensing Resources for Exact Time-II 59

8. Renewing Resources for Expectant Time-I 63

9. Renewing Resources for Expectant Time-II 72

10. God Ordering the Steps-and Stops-of a Good Man in Engineering Time-I 80

11. My Surrendering My Success Choices to His Sovereignty in Engineering Time-II 88

Part III: Practicing Prayer Power

12. DISCO (1) DIScerning the Demand 93

13. DISCO (2) Claiming the Promise 101

14. DISCO (3) Accessing Own Resources 110

15. LISCO (1) LIStening to the Lord 115

16. LISCO (2) Communicating the Message 127

17. LISCO (3) Offering Thanks 134

Answered prayers by concrete need 139

1

Practicing Prayer Power

It is the Lord's commitment: "I will do whatever you ask in my name" (John 14:13, NIV) that we invoke when we pray for concrete needs of ours and others. That invocation transcends common sense. This transcendence is seen from an example in the New Testament, and two real-life experiences in 1993.

How many times have you said to someone: "I will pray for you"? Think of the last time you said that. What did he or she expect? That his or her need would be fully met, just as desired? Or, at least partially met? Or did he or she think: "Oh, this prayer won't help; but it won't hurt either. Why not be safe and have someone say a prayer? In other words, a *spiritual bromide*.

Expecting resources to meet concrete need

That is not what the man, crippled from birth, thought when he saw one afternoon. Peter and John entering the temple. He could not get to the temple on his own; somebody had to carry him every day so that he could sit and beg alms from the worshippers. When he saw Peter and John about to enter the temple, he asked them for what he needed most: money.

Now, Peter had no money. He was the one who told Jesus: "But look, we have left all we had to follow you!" (Mark 10:28 PHI, MOF) Left *all we had* – our jobs as fishermen; our fishing nets; our worldly possessions. Not a drachma, not a red cent to our name!

Yet, the crippled beggar expected money from them, just as those who ask us to pray for their needs should expect to receive health, money, or jobs from God through our prayer for them – our intercessory prayer. "Peter looked straight at him as did John. Then Peter said, 'Look at us!' So the man gave them his attention, expecting to get something from them. Then Peter said, 'Silver or gold I do not have, but what I have I give to you. In the name of Jesus Christ of Nazareth, walk.'" (Acts 3:4-6)

Impossible! He had never walked in forty years! Yet Peter who was neither orthopedist nor physical therapist, told the man: **"Walk"** He did not say, "I hope that God will give you some money – I sure don't have any." He did not say: "I hope God will heal you so that some day you can walk on crutches, instead of having to be carried on someone's back all the time" No, he dared the impossible: **"Walk!"** and started to help the man up. "At once his feet and ankle bones were strengthened, and he sprang to his feet, stood, and then started to walk…leaping and praising God." (Acts 3:7-8, PHI, MOF)

The crippled beggar had a concrete physical need and a concrete financial need. He asked Peter to meet his urgent financial need. Instead, God met his important physical need. God "is able to do immeasurably more than all we ask or imagine, according to his power." (Ephesians 3:20)

#1 Answered professional need: Finding a new high-salary job quickly in a tight market—1993

At Fourth Presbyterian Church in Bethesda, Maryland, we have a men's prayer breakfast every other Tuesday. We have a prayer request form with five categories of needs: financial, physical, professional, relational, or spiritual. The request can be made anonymously – for one's self, friends, family or even foes! (Fig 1.1). We have experienced God's answer to concrete needs through specific Scriptures.

In Palestine, in A.D. 32, Jesus told the 70: "Don't carry a purse or a bag or a pair of shoes" (Luke 10:4, PHI) What relevance can this have in 1993 to a senior professional at Fourth, suddenly out of a job ?

One Tuesday morning, he wrote: "Need a job" on our prayer request form, signed his name, and handed it to me. (He could also have written the prayer request anonymously, and left it at the table, and nobody would have known his identity.) He is a man of great reserve; so his declaring in public that he needed a job showed how desperate he was. He calculated that it takes a month of job-hunting for each $10,000 in salary, and that he would need a year to find a job. I asked a friend to be his intercessor. In two weeks the intercessor received the message: Luke 10:1-5; and in 2½ months the professional got a wonderful job – in 80% less time than he expected.

Asking "in my name"

"I will do *whatsoever* you ask in my name." The Lord's promise is *un*conditional: no ifs; no buts. The only requirement is that it should be "In my name." How do we know that we are asking "In my name"? One way is to receive a scripture from the Lord to meet the concrete intercessory need.

But when you pray for a six-figure salary job for someone, what kind of an answer is it to say that Christ sent out the 70 with no purse, no bag and no shoes? So, if the intercessor picks what he thinks is a more helpful scripture like: "My God shall supply all your need"(Philippians 4:19, KJV), it is as dead as a doornail; it has no power. But when the Lord

Men of Fourth Ministry
Prayer Bulletin

Intercessory Prayer Requests by Concrete Need

At the Men's Retreat, March 1992, 60 men signed up to pray in pairs for concrete needs by Need Category: Physical (10); Professional (20); Relationship (12); Spiritual (18). Beginning Tuesday, December 15, 1992, we will receive intercessory prayer requests by concrete need for inclusion in the PRAYER BULLETIN (Editor: Doug Smoot) for the following Tuesday Prayer Breakfast.

On this Sheet please write down your request by need category. You can identify the person in need by first name, or use a made-up name within quotation marks "......" to preserve anonymity.

Financial CONCRETE Need:

Physical CONCRETE Need:

Professional CONCRETE Need

Relationship CONCRETE Need

Spiritual CONCRETE Need

We KNOW that our prayers are answered. Please enter here your Identified Answers for CONCRETE Need. Include any Scripture which was used by the Lord in answering your concrete need.

Thank you!

Fig. 1.1

gives the message, it speaks to the recipient – as it did to our professional seeking the job.

It is a rare privilege to be an intercessor, to bring someone's need before the Lord, and to receive a message in answer. Let me discuss the five steps of intercession expressed as the acronym: DEAVECO.

Intercessory step 1: D: Discern the demand

Are you the one to pray for this need at this time? Notice that the professional handed his prayer request to me, but I did not feel called upon by the Lord to intercede for him. Instead, the Lord directed me to my friend to handle the overwhelming need for a six-figure salary job. "The harvest truly is plenteous," but the Lord did not say: Therefore, rush into the harvest. He did not even say: Pray that you may be sent to the harvest. What he said was: "Pray ye therefore the Lord of the harvest that he will send forth laborers into his harvest" (Matthew 9:37-38, KJV) This might or might not be you. *If* you are chosen by the Lord to intercede, pray until you get a message from the Lord to meet the need.

Intercessory step 2: E :Empathize with the intercessee

The purpose of the intercession is not to tell the Lord what he should do and how, but to identify with God's interest in the situation. You must feel the intercessee's pain and ask the Lord for relief. The Lord may not give relief; Paul himself prayed the Lord three times to remove the thorn in his flesh (2 Corinthians 12:7-8, KJV) but it was not removed.

Intercessory step 3: A: Ask the Lord for a message

Quiet yourself before the Lord. Resist the temptation to reach for a comforting message, such as "My Lord shall supply all your need." Wait upon the Lord for his message.

#2 Answered physical need: Recovery of teenager found motionless in swimming pool—1993

When my wife and I and arrived in Taipei in August 1993, a missionary family urged us to stay with them for a few days. At suppertime the second day, our host shared a fax he received. The teenage son of a fellow-missionary in Hong Kong, a good swimmer, was found motionless in the swimming pool. Nobody knew how long he had been in the water, and how serious his brain injuries were. They had flown him to a good children's hospital in the Midwest in the United States. Would we pray for him? I did not know the missionary family; so I was a bystander who supported our host in his prayer.

That night around 12:40 A.M., when I remembered the teenager in my prayer, a phrase came to mind clear as a bell. I had not seen that phrase for fifty years. It was: "Tabitha koomi." Tabitha, we read in Acts 9, was a woman full of good works. She died and her washed body was laid in the upper room. They sent for Peter who was in the nearby town. "Peter... kneeled down, and prayed: and turning toward the dead woman, he said, 'Tabitha, get up.' And she opened her eyes; and when she saw Peter, she sat up." (Acts 9:40, KJV, NIV).

I was astonished that the Lord was choosing me as the intercessor for the teenager who was suspected to have suffered serious brain damage. At suppertime, I had passively joined the prayer; but by midnight I was thrust into active intercession. The Scripture I received was so astounding that I was scared. But the same message repeated itself unbidden eight or nine times in the next twelve hours. I gave the message to my host around 1 P.M. He faxed it to the parents. Two days later, we had a fax saying that there seemed to be no serious injury. A week later, the teenager was pronounced fully fit.

Intercessory step 4: VE: VErify the message

I follow *Gideon's Rule* to make sure that the message is the Lord's, and not the result of my sympathies for the intercessee. When Gideon, who was hiding his wheat crop from the plundering Midianites, was told to go and conquer them, it was so preposterous that Gideon tested the call three times. I wait to see if the identical message comes to me three or more times unbidden – when my thoughts are far away from the situation.

Intercessory step 5: CO: COmmunicate without comment

If it comes unbidden three or more times, then I ask the Lord *how and when* I should communicate the message. I do not edit, annotate, or interpret. That is between the recipient and the Lord. I tell him or her to ask the Lord what the message means, and what he or she should do. My job as messenger is done when I have communicated the message. How do I know that it was from the Lord? When the message makes sense to the recipient.

DEAVECO

The five intercessory steps can be made into an acronym: DEAVECO. **d**iscern the demand; empathize with the intercessee; ask the Lord for a promise; verify the promise; communicate without comment.

IF the Lord asks you to intercede for someone, pray until you get a message; transmit it. The Lord will bless him or her and you. Ascribe Him glory.

Ascription

"Now unto him who is able to keep [us] from falling and to present [us] spotless before the presence of his glory with exceeding joy, to the only wise God our Saviour, be glory and majesty, dominion and power, before all time, now and for evermore. Amen." (Jude 24-5,KJV, NEB, NIV).

Specific scriptural messages transcending common sense

Neither Acts 9:40 nor Luke 10:4 were "commonsense" answers to the exceptionally critical financial and physical problems – of having to find a six-figure salary job, and of receiving life back for the teenager. The messages confirmed that the prayers were "In His Name." The verification came when the specific Scripture spoke to the specific concrete need of the recipient.

Receiving the scripture from the Lord

It is the Lord who decides when and to whom He would give a specific Scripture to meet a concrete need. Boy Samuel, aged 5 or 6, did not ask the Lord for a message about his boss Eli's family. In fact, "Samuel did not yet know the Lord." (1 Samuel 3:7, NIV). Yet, the Lord chose to give him a message about the future of Eli's family. He answered: "Speak, Lord, for your servant is listening. (1 Samuel 3:9, NIV)

Can the Lord call us at midnight or 3 A.M. to give us a message for a concrete need? Will we answer, as Samuel did?

Prayer power workshop on DEAVECO

How do we start?

We can start with instances of answered prayer. To protect anonymity, you may want to use made-up names like "Joe" and "Jane" if your testimony could hurt or embarrass someone else.

What did you do? *How* did you pray? That would help others most.

Did you receive a Scripture to meet the concrete need? If you received the message from the Lord, how did you know that it was from the Lord? One test is that the message spoke to the recipient. You are only a messenger who, like the mailman, delivers an unopened piece of mail to the addressee. The message is from the Lord to the recipient. You do not read it; you do not interpret it.

What interpretation could my friend possibly have given the person who was looking for a job when the message spoke of the 70 being sent without a purse, without shoes, without a change of clothes? Should he give up everything and become an itinerant preacher? My friend was wise in faithfully transmitting the Lord's message, without second-guessing the Lord. The job-seeker's response was: "My wife and I have been reading Luke. We are at chapter 8. But we will jump ahead to chapter 10."

Prayer Power Partnership (P-Cubed)
Two-Minute Testimony Worksheet

OBJECTIVE: Tell someone with a similar need how God answered you.

TYPE OF NEED: My need was primarily (Check One): (1) Financial, (2) Physical, (3) Professional, (4) Relational, or (5) Spiritual.

PERSON(S) INVOLVED: The need involved (Check One): (1) Myself, (2) Myself and one other person, (3) Myself and two or more, (4) Only others.

BRIEF DESCRIPTION: Use made-up names like "Joe" and "Jane" if your testimony could embarrass/hurt others. Respect privacy – your own and other people's. We want to glorify God, not hurt man (woman). (1) What was the particular need? (2) When? (3) Why was it a problem?(4) Were you hard-pressed to find an answer? (5) Were others aware of your problem?

WHAT DID YOU DO?: Did you pray? HOW did you pray? (This is most helpful to someone facing a similar situation).

DID YOU CLAIM A PROMISE?"I will do whatever you ask in my name." (John 14:13) "Whatever" has no caveats. Did you feel that your need would be met, although you had no way of knowing how it would be met? Was it just a hope that somehow things would work out; or was it something definite? Did the experience with this need situation change your understanding of John 14:13?

HOW DID YOU "ASK IN MY NAME?" One way to make sure that what we ask is "In His Name", or according to His Will, is to receive a Scripture from the Lord – Not closing your eyes and putting your finger blindly on a page of Scripture!

INVOKING PROMISE: If you received a Scripture as God's promise to your need, was it of the type: Lord, because you said (did) ..., would you do ... ?

IMPLEMENTING PROMISE: Or was the promise of the type:"Take the first fish you catch; open its mouth and you will find a four-drachma coin."(Matt 17:27)?

HOW DID YOU RECOGNIZE YOUR PROMISE: (1) Your own positive assurance, (2) Confirmation by others, (2) Confirmation by events/relationships

HOW WAS YOUR NEED MET?: Briefly state the particulars; Respect privacy.

LESSONS LEARNED: Did a particular Scripture become more real to you after the need was met than before? Did you doubt? Do say so if you did. Did someone else say something which helped you?

PRAYER POWER PARTNERSHIP: Prayer having met your need, would you help someone else in a similar need situation of need? Thank you!

The Lord's blessings on your ministry of intercession!

Fig. 1.2

Two-minute testimony

In Fig. 1.2 we have a two-minute testimony worksheet. The reason why the time is limited to two minutes is because the discipline and preparation to give a two-minute testimony would focus one's attention on receiving a message from the Lord for oneself, one's family, or others. If you haven't received a message as the answer, but have witnessed answered prayers, praise the Lord for what He has done, and look to Him to show you the next step.

> KEY WORDS/PHRASES:
> Spiritual bromide; concrete needs; "Whatsoever you ask in my name; Gideon's rule; communicating without comment.

Discussion Starters- Chapter 1

1. What was the urgent need of the beggar at the Temple; what was his important need?

2. What should someone requesting your prayer expect?

3. How do you know that you are praying "In His Name"?

4. A situation for which you have a burden right now. Are you called to be the intercessor, or for passive prayer?

5. Briefly specify the 5 steps of DEAVECO.

6. Review the 5 KEY WORDS/PHRASES:
Spiritual bromide; concrete needs; "Whatsoever you ask in my name;" Gideon's rule; communicating without comment.

2

Claiming the Lord's Commitment

It is the Lord's commitment: "I will do whatsoever you ask in my name," that we invoke when we pray for concrete needs of ours and others. That invocation transcends common sense. This transcendence is seen from an example in the Old Testament, and two in the New Testament in Chapter 2. What are the essential elements of the miracles transcending the rational; what do they teach us about developing an appropriate persistent perspective profile? The transcendence in time in answered prayer is discussed in chapter 3.

"Remember, I am with you always, even to the end of the world." (Matthew 28:20, PHI)

The Risen Lord, triumphant over sin and death, announces as He transcends time and space, that He is ever-present with those who trust in Him, always. Always means everywhere, anytime. Eternal contemporaneousness is a mouthful, but it means that the Lord is contemporary, here and now, with us in our current situation; and that the Lord is contemporary forever, be it in A.D. 33 or B.C. 1206; be it in Jerusalem or Washington, DC. The Lord with us now.

If the Lord really is with us, why has all this happened to us? (Judges 6:13, NEB)

If the Lord is with us now, in the present situation, why it is so bad? This question is as natural in the 1990s as it was 3,100 years ago, in B.C. 1206. In fact, that is exactly how a dispirited Israelite, beating out some wheat inside a winepress to quickly get it away from the raiders, phrases his question. For seven years, Midianites starved out the Israelites. "Whenever Israel had sown their crops, Midian and Amalek and the Bedawin would come up raiding, and ruined the crops as far south as Gaza and

[left] nothing to support life in Israel, neither sheep nor cattle nor donkeys." (Judges 6: 3-4, MOF, NIV) With "nothing to support life," without food and meat, how could Israel survive? The Israelites cried out to the Lord who sent them a prophet who recounted God's faithfulness and Israel's faithlessness. God rescued them from Egypt and gave them the land of their enemies, but instead of worshipping God, they worshiped gods of the Amorites, disobeying the commandments: "I am the Lord thy God.... Thou shalt have no other gods but me." (Exodus 20: 2,3, KJV, MOF)

Enter an angel. He visits Gideon in his valley of humiliation, precisely where and when he is hurting. His greeting of the cowering Gideon is astounding: "The Lord is with you, mighty warrior." (Judges 6:12, NIV) Gideon elaborates how unmighty a warrior he is, hailing from the weakest clan, carrying the least weight in his family. Yes, the Lord was with my fathers, so they tell us. They talk of a God who worked wonders against all odds, but where is He now? He no longer cares for us, and has thrown us to the Midianites. How could Gideon dream of becoming a conquering hero, when for seven years, the whole might of Israel was of no avail against the Midianites?

The comission to do the impossible—(1) Save Israel from Midian

Right in the midst of Gideon's hopelessness comes the Lord's commission to do the impossible: "Go in the strength you have and save Israel out of Midian's hand. Am I not sending you? ... I will be with you, and you shall smite the Midianites as one man." (Judges 6: 14,16, NIV, KJV) Eternal contemporaneousness is not the absence of troubles, but the presence of the Lord in their midst. God does not keep us from the fire, He walks with us in the fire: "Then King Nebuchadnezzar leaped to his feet in amazement [and said], "Look! I see four men walking around in the fire, unbound and unharmed, and the fourth looks like the Son of God." (Daniel 3: 24,25, NIV, KJV)

Empowering Presence Alone Sufficient for Smashing Victory

"The strength you have" is what God uses to meet His specific commission to Gideon: "Save Israel out of Midian's hand." What makes Gideon a majority of one is the presence of the Lord with him: "I will be with you."

Drastic Downsizing to Deny Any Claims of Human Victory

Over 135,000 armed men lay in wait for Israel under Gideon, who mustered about 32,000. But God wanted Gideon to drastically downsize his army from 32,000 to 300, so that Israel would not boast of her own strength. When one Israelite fights against 450 Midianites, even by the farthest stretch of the imagination, victory could not have come from Israel's might.

The commission to do the impossible – (2) Feed 5,000; Feed 4,000

Defeating an army 450 times as large is inconceivable, particularly by someone who has no military credentials. How much more inconceivable is the carrying out of the command to twelve men who had left everything to follow Jesus to feed two masses of five thousand and of the four thousand?

Implausibility No. 1: No fast-food or even slow-food facilities

The setting is "the wilderness." No fast-food places, no McDonald's, not even slow-food places in sight. "As evening fell his disciples came to him and said, 'We are right in the wilds here and it is very late. Send away these crowds now, so that they can go into the villages and buy themselves food.'" (Matthew 14:15, PHI)

Implausibility No. 2: Extremely fatigued masses of families

The people have been in the wilderness for a whole day in one instance and for three days in another. How do you get food and drink in the desert? You carry supplies – things that keep in hot weather. Few could afford to carry three days' supplies for their families – husband, wife, two or more children: total provision for (5,000 x 4 =) 20,000. After three days the crowds were extremely fatigued. "Jesus called his disciples to him and said, "I have compassion for these people; they have already been with me three days and have nothing to eat. I do not want to send them away hungry, or they may collapse on the way." (Matthew 15:32, NIV)

Implausibility No. 3: The huge magnitude of the need

By the third day, any supplies that the people had brought would have been exhausted. How much food was needed? One loaf per family would require 5,000 loaves; two per family, 10,000; and three per family, 15,000 loaves.

Implausibility No. 4: No money, no assets

At $1.50 a loaf, 15,000 cost $22,500. The twelve disciples have only minimal assets, and feeding the crowds would take more than eight months' wages.

Implausibility No. 5: Pauper-Disciples Feeding Five Thousand Families

Those with no assets could not come up with $22,500 right on the spot. Yet Jesus said: "Give ye them to eat." (Matthew 14:16, KJV) The command was no less specific nor less daring than the angel's command to Gideon: "Save Israel out of Midian's hand." Knowing that the disciples had no resources to meet the vast material need of the starving masses, Jesus says "You give them something to eat!" (Matthew 14:16, PHI)

Faith step one: Access your own resources, however meager

The disciples did not have the required $22,500. In fact, they did not have any food of their own. Yet Jesus asks: "How many loaves do you have?" (Matthew 15:34, NIV) Andrew, in the Gospel of John, says who the donor of sandwiches was: "'There is a boy here who has five barley loaves and two fishes; but what is that among so many?'" (John 6:8-9, NEB)

Faith step two: Offer your own resources to the Lord

They were right; their resources were far too small to meet the need. Yet Jesus says: one, access your resources (How many loaves do you have?); two, offer them to the Lord. "He said, 'Bring them here to me.'" (Matthew 14: 18, MOF) The boy was willing to give up his entire lunch. Andrew told him, "The Lord hath need of them." (Matthew 21:3, KJV)

Faith step three: The offered resource used to meet the pressing need

"And when he had taken the five loaves and the two fishes, he [1] looked up to heaven, and [2] blessed, and [3] brake the loaves, and [4] gave them to his disciples to [5] distribute to the people." (Mark 6:41, KJV, PHI) The willingness of the boy to give up his claim to his possession and place it in the Lord's hand gave the Lord the opportunity to use it to meet the boy's own needs, and those of 5,000 families. This miraculous transformation of the private gift into public fulfillment comprises five elements. (See Chapter 4 for further discussion of what constitutes a miracle.)

Miracle element (1) divine dependence – Looking up to heaven

There are three recorded occasions when Jesus looked up to heaven: (1) the feeding of the five thousand, (2) the healing the deaf and near-mute (Mark 7:34) and (3) the farewell discourses in the Upper Room. (John 17:1) Looking toward heaven or spreading one's hands toward heaven is to both affirm God's power and to invoke His providence: *divine dependence.*

We see Moses and Solomon practicing it. The Pharaoh asked Moses to beseech the Lord to stop the plague of thunder and hail: "And Moses went out of the city from Pharaoh, and spread abroad his hands unto the Lord: and the thunders and hail ceased, and the rain was not poured upon the earth" (Exodus 9:33, KJV). At the dedication of the Temple, "Solomon stood before the altar of the Lord in the presence of all the congregation of Israel, and spread forth his hands toward heaven" (1 Kings 8:22, KJV).

Miracle element (2) divine access – Blessing the gift of bread and fishes

Looking up to heaven Jesus blessed what the boy offered, invoking the divine favor, for a specific purpose: Feeding the five thousand.

Blessing can also be the assurance of divine favor in general, as when Isaac gave his blessings to Esau and Jacob. The importance of the paternal blessing is seen from Esau's anguished outcry to Isaac: "Hast thou not reserved a blessing for me?" (Genesis 27:36, KJV) Paternal blessing is most powerful since it is prescient and pervasive as Isaac's blessing of Jacob demonstrates: "I have made him lord over you and have made all his relatives his servants, and I have sustained him with grain and new wine." Perhaps the most powerful of all blessings is God's blessing of Abraham: "Thou shalt be a blessing"(Genesis 12:2, KJV). Note how great Abraham's blessing was: "I will make you into a great nation, I will bless you and make your name so great that it shall be used in blessings." (Genesis 12:2, NEB) And we see that Isaac himself uses his father's name to bless Jacob: "And God Almighty bless thee, ... and give thee the blessing of Abraham to thee, and to thy seed with thee." (Genesis 28:3-4, KJV).

Miracle element (3) resource generation – Multiplying the gift of bread, fish

In looking up to heaven and blessing the boy's offering, Jesus was invoking God's commitment to meet our concrete needs: "My God will supply all your own needs from his wealth in Glory in Christ Jesus." (Phil 4:19, MOF) To supply the need for food for more than 5,000, the loaves and fish had to be multiplied some 3,000 times – something beyond all human capabilities.

When Elijah hid from King Ahab, he stayed near a brook. When it ran dry due to the continuing drought, Elijah was sent to the widow of Zarephath of Sidon. He asks her for a drink of water (quite difficult due to prolonged drought), and then for a piece of bread. She says that she has no bread, but "only a handful of flour in a jar and a little oil in a jug. I am gathering a few sticks to take home and make a meal for myself and my son, that we may eat it-and die." (1 Kings 17:12, NIV) She brings to Elijah her very last meal. She has nothing left. Giving up the very last morsel that she and her son have on the earth means that they are choosing to die starving. Yet that very self-effacing gift is blessed to multiply into daily bread for three persons for one-two years.

Miracle element (4) care conveyors – Giving it to the disciples

The single lunch given up by the anonymous boy was multiplied into a veritable mountain of food. To distribute it to 5,000 families, the 12 disciples would have to press into service many volunteers: *Resource conveyors.*

Resource conveyors were required in the early church to rectify the complaint that the widows of the Grecian Jews were being overlooked in the daily distribution of food. "So the Twelve called the whole body of disciples together and said, 'It would be a grave mistake for us to neglect preaching the Word of God in order to wait on tables. You, our brothers, must look round and pick out from your number seven men of good reputation who are both practical and spiritually-minded and we will put them in charge of this matter. Then we shall devote ourselves wholeheartedly to prayer and the ministry of the Word.'" (Acts 6:2-4, NEB, PHI)

Resource conveyors are needed in matters of food (physical), as well as in matters of administering justice (non-physical): Collectively we may call them *care conveyors*. Jethro, Moses' father-in-law, asked why Moses was wearing himself out trying to arbitrate between disputants all day long. 'The people come to me,' Moses answered, 'to seek God's guidance. Whenever there is a a dispute among them, they come to me, and I decide between man and man. I declare the statutes and laws of God." (Exodus 18:15-16, NEB) Jethro advises Moses to delegate: "You must yourself search for some capable men among the people, religious men, honest men, who scorn unjust profits, and appoint them to supervise groups of thousands, of hundreds, of fifties, and of tens. They shall sit as a permanent court for the people in ordinary cases; they can refer any special case to you, and judge lesser matters by themselves." (Exodus 18: 21-22, NEB, MOF)

Miracle element (5) need fulfillment – Giving it to the people

The miracle started with a pressing need, to meet which someone offered his meager resources. Jesus invoked God's power to multiply the resources manyfold and gave them to the disciples, who engaged a volunteer army of care conveyors to reach the people in need.

God meets needs abundantly when the best human guess can only despair: "Philip answered Jesus, 'Eight months' wages would not buy enough bread for each one to have a bite." (John 6:7, NIV) But the Psalmist knew better. He says that the children of men who put their trust under the shadow of thy wings "shall be abundantly satisfied with the fatness of thy house; and thou shalt make them drink of the river of thy pleasures." (Psalm 36:8, KJV) No matter the type of need – physical, mental, spiritual – God provides abundantly: "Now unto Him who is able to do exceedingly abundantly, aye far more than we can ever ask or imagine" (Ephesians 3:20, KJV, MOF) God fulfills our needs way beyond our wildest imagination!

Dare we trust that He is able?

The signed blank check given to us is exhilarating when we venture out in the faith that there are adequate resources to fully meet our present concrete need right now. However, right after a dramatic demonstration of God's provisions for the concrete need for food of the five thousand, as the disciples are crossing the lake, there comes a test of their faith. Could He who fed the 5,000 quiet the raging sea?

"What made you lose your nerve like that?"

Immediately after feeding the 5,000, Jesus sent his disciples to the other side of the lake ahead of him, and went up the hillside to pray alone:

> The boat was already some furlongs from the shore, battling with a head-wind and a rough sea. Between three and six in the morning he came to them, walking over the lake. When the disciples saw him walking on the lake, they were so shaken that they cried out in terror: "It is a ghost!" But at once Jesus spoke to them, "It's alright! It's I myself, don't be afraid!" Peter answered him, "Lord, if is really you, order me to come to you on the water." He said, "Come." Peter stepped down from the boat and began to walk over the water toward Jesus. But when he saw the fury of the wind, he panicked and began to sink. "Lord," he shouted, "save me." At once Jesus stretched his hand out and caught him, saying, "How little you trust me! What made you lose your nerve like that?" Then, when they both got into the boat, the wind dropped, and the men in the boat fell at his feet, exclaiming. "Truly you are indeed the Son of God!" (Matthew 14:24-33, NEB,PHI,MOF)

Beyond common sense

We have to be realistic in facing our problems, be it the raging sea or the famished five thousand. Philip saw how vast the problem was to feed 5,000: "Philip answered [Jesus], 'Eight months' wages would not buy enough bread for each one to have a bite." If Philip were realistic, Andrew was pragmatic. Andrew looked around for anything that could conceivably help with the problem, and he identified perhaps the only accessible resource. "One of his disciples, Andrew, the brother of Simon Peter, said to him, 'There is a boy here who has five barley loaves and two fishes; but what is that among so many?'"But neither the realist nor the pragmatist could even dream the miraculous solution which defied realism and pragmatism.

In crossing the lake, Peter, a fisherman, knew the serious problem: the boat was battling with a headwind and a rough sea for a good part of the night, and it was now 4 or 5 A.M.. But if Jesus can walk over the turbulent sea, why can't I, Peter, also walk over water? Jesus asks Peter to step out on his faith. He does fine, as long as his eyes are on Jesus; but, then, common sense sets in: What about the raging headwind that is tossing the whole boat? He looks at the problem, and forgets the One who was looking at it with him. He forgets that the One who told him to step out on faith rules the waves and the sea. The problem overwhelms Peter; he sinks. As he sinks, he shouts: "Lord, save me!" And he is saved. How can the experience of one miracle (physical: feeding of the 5,000) sustain in us in another (spiritual: walking on water)?

Persistent perspective profile

As long as Peter's eyes were focused on the Master's command: "Come [over the water]", Peter walked on water with abandon. The moment his eyes were focused on the problem perspective, he began to sink. The only way he could keep from sinking is to maintain his perspective persistently.

Persistent perspective profile element: (1) Person

What is the problem? Able fisherman that he was, Peter noticed that the sea was raging into the small hours of the morning. He could never solve the problem-calm the sea; he could at best cope with it – by keeping the boat afloat.

Suddenly he sees an incredible victory over the problem itself. Jesus does not stop the waves; He walks over them. That is exciting, and Peter wants to duplicate what the Master did. He does not jump out, but asks the Master to order him to walk over the water. He is commanded to do so. Peter jumps out knowing that Jesus would give him the power to cope with the horrendous problem. As Shadrach, Meshach, and Abednego found out in B.C. 580, God does not save us from the fire but walks with us in the fire. What Peter needed then, and what we need today, is to keep looking at the One who said He will be with us in the present, concrete problem: *Persistent perspective of the Person.* "Surrounded as we are by these serried ranks of witnesses, let us throw off everything that hinders and every clinging sin and let us run with perseverance the race marked out for us, our eyes fixed upon Jesus, the author and perfecter of our faith " (Hebrews 12: 1-2, PHI,NEB,NIV)

Persistent perspective profile element: (2) Plan

The author of Hebrews tells us to run with perseverance. How? By persisting in the race marked out for us. The race is well marked out with a well understood starting point, a well specified course, and a well understood ending point. But the race of life has only a well understood starting point: Birth; both the course and the ending point are unique to each person.

If we do not know what the course is, how can we persevere in it? The cynic may well say: If you don't know where you are going, any road will take you there. We answer: We know why we are going, therefore, the why determines the what and the how for us:

> Here and now, my dear friends, we are God's children, and what we shall become in the future has not yet been made known, but we know that when he appears we are to be like him-for we are to see him as he is! (1 John 3:2, PHI, NIV, MOF)

To John, the chief end of life is the ability to see Him face to face, as it is for Paul. Paul's great ambition is to know (now) and attain resurrection (later): "I want to know Christ and the power of his resurrection...[and] to attain the resurrection from the dead: (Philippians 3:10-11, NIV, PHI) Given the goal, Paul strives to reach it:

> But one thing I do: Forgetting what is behind and straining toward what is ahead, I press on toward the goal to win the prize which is God's call to the life above, in Christ Jesus (emphasis added). (Philippians 3:13-14 , NIV, NEB)

Now we have specified two points of the race of life: (1) The starting point: Birth, and (2) The ending point: Life above. How do we run with perseverance the race marked out for us? Run the race so that the mortal life obtained at birth is transformed into the eternal life at the ending point:

> But we all mirror the glory [splendor] of the Lord with face unveiled, and so we are being transformed [transfigured] into the same likeness as himself, passing from one glory to another [from splendor to splendor], which is the work of the Lord, who is the Spirit (2 Corinthians 3:18, MOF, NIV, NEB)

Notice that neither John nor Paul knows what awaits him: "What we shall become in the future has not yet been made known," says John; "Forgetting what is behind and straining toward what is ahead," says Paul. He does not know what he will become; but he does know why: "I press on, hoping to take hold of that for which Christ once took hold of me" (Philippians 3:12, NEB), or as Phillips pus it: "I keep going on, trying to grasp the purpose for which Christ Jesus grasped me." (Philippians 3:12, PHI)

It is the Person that determines the Plan. Christ has a purpose for me; I strive to fulfill it. How do I persist in the right direction?

Persistent perspective profile element: (3) Prayer-Personal

We find that Jesus was persistent in his prayer. Right after feeding the

5,000, he sends the multitude and his disciples away so that he can pray by himself: "And when he had sent them away he went up the hill-side quite alone, to pray." (Matthew 14:23, PHI) Notice that he had prayed alone most of the night; it was not until 4 or 5 A.M. that he walked over the water toward the boat.

To Christ, prayer is communion with the Father. We see that the chief end of prayer is our relationship with the Father, any results being a token of the relationship. He underscores the primacy of the relationship over results when the seventy came back with joy and reported that the very demons obeyed them in Christ's name. He replies:

> Rejoice not because the spirits obey you:
> rejoice because your names are enrolled in heaven.
> (Luke 10:20, MOF)

Enrollment of their names in heaven signifies eternal life with the Father, which is far more important than the submitting of the demons to the power of God the seventy invoked. Clearly, subduing the demons was an imperative need for their mission as advance team for Jesus's subsequent visit to the towns he intended to visit himself. But he wanted them to rely on the heavenly Father's knowledge of their needs beforehand, and to pray for their needs with assurance: "[D]o not keep on babbling like pagans who think they will be heard because they use so many words. You must not copy them; your Father knows what you need before you ask him." (Matthew 6:7-8, NIV, MOF, PHI)

Persistent perspective profile element: (4) Prayer-Intercessory
While the Father knows beforehand what you need, He nevertheless wants you to ask Him for your needs; and He wants others to ask Him for you. What is the first recorded intercession in the Bible? It is easy to miss it because the word intercede appears only in Moffatt's translation, even the NIV rendering it as "pray."

#3. Answered physical need: God curing a king – B.C. 1807 (Expectant time)

The king woke up shuddering at the nightmare. He had gone to sleep, happy at the prospect of enjoying the beautiful sister of the wealthy visitor to his country. "You are a dead man; for this woman whom you have taken is a married woman," (Genesis 20:3, MOF) the king was told in his dream. "Lord, wilt thou slay innocent folk? Did he not tell me himself, 'She is my sister,' and she herself said, 'He is my brother?' I did it in all simplicity and innocence." (Genesis 20:4-5, MOF) Accepting the protestations of innocence of King Abimelech of Gerar, the Lord says to him: "But now restore the man's wife – for he is a prophet and he will intercede for you, so that you may recover" (Genesis 20:7, MOF)

Intercessory Triangle:
God → Abimelech → Abram; Abram → God → Abimelech

We see that it is God who initiated the intercession. It was a particular person, Abraham, who interceded for a particular person, Abimelech. And it was God who provided an identified answer. Couldn't God have simply cut out the middleman, and forgiven Abimelech directly? Certainly, but we see that God chooses to bless the triangle formed by the intercessor Abram and intercessee Abimelech as the sides and God as the apex.

#4. Answered spiritual need: Christ restoring Peter – A.D. 33 (Expectant Time)

From the Old Testament, we turn to the New Testament.

Intercessory Triangle: God → Jesus → Peter

Jesus himself intercedes for us without our even knowing about it: "Simon, Simon, Satan has claimed the right to sift you all like wheat, but I have prayed for you that you may not lose your own faith. And when you have turned back to me, you must strengthen these brothers of yours." (Luke 22:31-33, MOF, PHI) Again, couldn't God have simply cut out the middleman, and strengthened Peter directly? Certainly, but we see that God chooses to bless the triangle formed by the intercessor Jesus and intercessee Peter as the sides and God as the apex.

The answer to Jesus' intercession begins with Peter's agony of repentance: "Immediately the cock crew, and the words of Jesus came back into Peter's mind – 'Before the cock crows you will disown me three times.' And he went outside and wept bitterly." (Matthew 26:75, PHI)

#5. Answered spiritual need: Saul becoming Paul – A.D. 34 (Expectant Time)

From the restoration of Peter we turn to the conversion of Paul.

Intercessory Triangle: Saul → God → Ananias

The Jewish Christian Ananias was scared stiff at the news that "Saul, yet breathing threatenings and slaughter against the disciples of the Lord," (Acts 9:1, KJV) was on his way to Damascus. He had most probably barricaded himself inside his house. Now the Lord comes to him in a vision and asks him to go looking for the very murderous enemy.

Ananias protests to the Lord that Saul is in Damascus with authority "to put anyone in chains who invokes thy Name!" (Acts 9:14, MOF) Yet when told that he is the one who is to lay hands on Saul to bring back his sight, Ananias goes at considerable risk to his own life. He enters the house where Saul is praying, which is certainly contrary to public knowledge and to common sense! He lays "his hands on him with these words, "Saul, my brother, I have been sent by the Lord, by Jesus who appeared to you on the road, to let you regain your sight and be filled with the Holy Spirit." (Acts 9:17, MOF)

The God triangle

One good reason for God using the circuitous route of Intercessor ➔ God ➔ Intercessee, instead of the direct route of God ➔ Intercessee, is found in the Lord's Prayer, which begins with not "My Father," but "Our Father." When Ananias made himself available to God to reach Saul, a new community was born, a community in which arch-enemies Saul and Ananias could together say, "Our Father," and mean it in a manner impossible before.

Criss-crossing arrows

While the triangle always starts at the apex with God, the concrete need moves (1) from Intercessee (Saul) ➔ God; (2) direction from God ➔ Intercessor; protest (3) from Intercessor ➔ God; resolution (4) from God ➔ Intercessor; obedience (5) from intercessor ➔ intercessee.

Aren't we irrelevant?

It is God who initiates the intercession (Abimelech has to request Abram to intercede); it is God through Whom we intercede (Through Jesus Christ); and it is God who answers our intercession (God healing Abimelech and family). Aren't we irrelevant? Certainly not. God takes the long way around precisely because He wants to create a new community out of every intercession; and I am one side of the triangle as intercessee/intercessor. Oswald Chambers says:

> The Spirit of God needs the nature of the believer as a shrine in which to offer His intercession...[W]e do not so often realize that the Holy Spirit Himself prays in us prayers which we cannot utter....
>
> Your intercession can never be mine, and my intercessions can never be yours, but the Holy Ghost

> makes intercession in our particular lives, without which intercession someone will be impoverished (*My Utmost for His Highest*, Simpkin Marshall, London, 1942, pp. 312-3).

May we be available to the Lord for the Spirit to make intercession, for we do not even know what we ought to pray for (what it is right to pray for), but the Spirit within us himself actually intercedes for us with groanings which cannot be uttered.

KEY WORDS: The God Triangle; Faith Steps; Miracle Elements; Persistent Perspective Profile Elements; Prayer Bulletin; Eternal contemporaneousness

Discussion Starters – Chapter 2

1. What is the highest Scriptural basis for intercession?

2. What is the first intercession in the Bible? Why doesn't God eliminate the middleman (woman) and meet the need of the person directly?

3. Why did Jesus give the impossible commission: "You give them something to eat!"

4. What were the steps that converted the impossible into the possible?

5. What do the Persistent Perspective Profile elements accomplish?

6. Review the 5 KEY WORDS:
The God Triangle; Faith Steps; Miracle Elements; Persistent Perspective Profile Elements; Prayer Bulletin; Eternal contemporaneousness

Pray the Lord that you may find an intercessor for a concrete need of yours.

3

God's Provisioning In Exact Time And Expectant Time

The transcendence in time in answered prayer is discussed in chapter 3. God's message meeting our concrete need specifies its fulfillment in the future (expectant time) or in the immediate (exact time). We find expectant time in an answered prayer in the Old Testament. We find exact time in two miracles in the New Testament and two in 1955 and 1990. When we transmit God's messages, we function as angels, second class (ASC). What is more, we are witnessing to the resurrection power.

"I will show you what must happen in the future" (Rev. 4:1, PHI)

When we claim the Lord's commitment: "I will do whatsoever you ask in my name," we witness to the resurrection power.

Resurrection radiance – Transcending of dimensions

When God became man, He imposed upon Himself the human limitations of time and space. None of us can go through a concrete wall; none of us knows what will happen in the next moment. After his resurrection, Jesus did something He never did before: (1) He transcended space: "Late that Sunday evening, when the disciples were together behind locked doors, for fear of the Jews, Jesus entered and stood right in the middle of them;"(John 20:19, NEB, MOF, PHI) (2) He transcended time: When Mary Magdalene and the other Mary reached the sepulcher at dawn on Sunday, the angel told them that He was risen, and recalled what Jesus had said just before crucifixion,"But after I am risen again, I will go before you into Galilee," (Matthew 26:32, KJV) they "ran to give the news to his disciples. But quite suddenly, Jesus stood before them in their path, and said, "Peace be with you!" (Matthew 28:9, PHI) The risen

Lord, in visible human form, was no longer limited by space or time dimensions. The fundamental fact of resurrection is the transcending of dimensions – from the finite to the infinite.

Angels and their messages

The angel at the sepulcher tells the women that Jesus "goes before you into Galilee; you will see him there! Now I have told you my message." (That is my message for you.) (Matthew 28:7, PHI, MOF) True to his name, the angel gave a message from God, the word "angel" meaning messenger. Personal messages from God, specific as to time and place, are brought time and again in the Bible, by angels.

Expectant time

Expectant time is the future time frame of fulfillment of a divine message.

#6. Answered physical need: God giving Abram a son – B.C. 1897 (Expectant time)

At age 75, Abram was told to leave all that was near and dear to him, and go out into the unknown. He was given a great promise: He would be father of many nations. That was in B.C. 1921; and the present time is B.C. 1898, which is 23 years later, and no son has yet been born to his beloved Sarah! Here come three angels who bring a specific, personal message to meet a concrete need: "next spring [B.C. 1897]... your wife Sarah shall have a son." (Genesis 18:10, MOF)

The event is to take place nine months hence, making that a time of expectation: *expectant time*. We find similar messages in the New Testament: "Fear not Zacharias ... thy wife Elisabeth shall bear ... John." (Luke 1: 13, KJV) "Fear not Mary ... thou shalt conceive ... Jesus." (Luke 1:30-31, KJV)

Exact time

From three examples of expectant time, we turn to two instances of *exact time*. Exact time is the instantaneous timeframe of fulfillment of a divine message.

#7. Answered physical need: Christ restoring to life the dying son of a royal official – A.D. 30 (Exact time)

The royal official probably walked eight hours from Capernaum to Cana to reach Jesus and beg him to heal his son at the point of death. After meeting him, the official walks back for eight hours, when he is met by his servants:

> The royal official said, "Sir, please come down before my boy dies!" Jesus replied, "You may go. Your son will live." The man took Jesus at his word and departed. While he was still on the way, his servants met him with the news; "Your son is alive and well." So he asked them at what time he had begun to recover, and they replied: "The fever left him yesterday at one o'clock in the afternoon." Then the father realized that this was the *exact time* at which Jesus had said to him: "Your son will live" (emphasis added). (John 4: 49-53, NIV, PHI)

#8. Answered physical need: Christ healing the centurion's servant – A.D. 31 (Exact time)

A year later, Jesus was in Capernaum. A centurion beseeched him. "Lord," he said, "my servant lies at home paralyzed and in terrible suffering." Jesus said to him, "I will go and heal him." The centurion says that he does not deserve to have Jesus come under his roof. "But just say the word, and my servant will be healed." Jesus is astonished at the faith of the centurion and says: "Go! It will be done just as you believed it would." And his servant was healed at that actual moment. (Matthew 8:6-8;13, NIV, PHI)

God lifting the veil of time

When they appeared to Abram, to Zacharias, and to Mary, the angels were given a peek into the future – nine months ahead. They transcended both time and space to appear suddenly in front of Abram, Zacharias, and Mary. When the angel says: "I will show you what must happen in the future," he speaks in the same tradition of the angels who brought messages specific as to time and place. Who were the messengers: "Three men"; "Gabriel"; and "Angel Gabriel".

Although awesome, the personal messages, specific as to a time and place, brought by the messengers, offered the recipients a glimpse into the future. As finite beings, we do not know what will happen the very next moment. However, God is infinite, which means to Him, Yesterday = Today = Tomorrow. To us, Tomorrow is unseen and unseeable; but it is known to God. And if He chooses to lift the veil of time, and show us what is going to occur nine months hence, that message lets us transcend time and space either immediately (exact time) or eventually (expectant time).

This transcendence over time is not an everyday occurrence. Nor is it invoked as a plaything. Abram waited for 23 years before he was given a glimpse of the next nine months. That assured him of God's faithfulness toward the incredibly wondrous promise of making a 100-year-old man and his barren wife the parents of many nations.

The highest gift

Imagine the privilege of being God's messengers – bringing to specific persons particular announcements that make the most sense only to them. To be such an angel to Saul, the avowed anti-christian, was literally life-threatening to the chosen angel, Ananias; but he obeyed, and had the privilege of baptizing the missionary to the western world, Paul.

Phillips alone specifies what the highest gift is: "The highest gift you can wish for is to be able to speak the messages of God." (1 Corinthians 14:1) Note the plural: "messages." In the singular, there is only one message: "For God so loved the world, that he gave his only begotten Son, that whosoever believeth in him should not perish, but have everlasting life." (John 3:16, KJV) But Phillips talks not of the message, but of the messages. These messages are the ones that Abram, Zacharias, Mary and Saul received. To carry out the specific function of bringing God's messages to the particular person at the specific time and place, we can indeed become angels – messengers.

The Psalmist says: "For thou hast made him a little lower than the angels." (Psalm 8:5, KJV) In what sense are we lower? In the three instances of angels announcing births of sons nine months hence, the messengers transcended time by foreseeing nine months hence; they transcended space by appearing from nowhere. The transcending of space struck terror in the hearts of Zacharias and Mary whose Jewish upbringing associated the expulsion of Adam and Eve with such appearances. We human beings are not known to transcend space, although we can and do transcend time when bringing God's message to specific persons, foretelling events to take place many months and years hence: "Seven years of great abundance are coming throughout the land of Egypt, but seven years of famine will follow them"(Genesis 41: 29-30, NIV) As Angels, Second Class (ASC) we are privileged to transcend time, on occasion, but not space. Hence we are a little lower than the angels.

#9. Answered financial need: Seminary student meeting his tuition deadline – circa 1955 (exact time)

When we need some specific resource to meet a pressing need at a particular time, can our request sound like anything but an "ultimatum'? The Rev. Frank Hartsell, retired Air Force Chaplain, tells of a seminary student whose widowed mother had run out of all her resources to pay his tuition. There was not a single penny in her cookie jar! The student in his second year at the seminary had exhausted all possible sources of aid. And, dreading the bleak prospects of not having the resources to continue his studies, prayed: "Lord, I need the money to pay the tuition by 2:30 P.M. today, or I will have to leave the seminary."

That "ultimatum" was very much like Peter's need for money to pay the temple tax. Peter had the Lord with him in body; the seminary student did not. The odds against his getting the large sum of money were similar to those of Peter finding the temple tax in the mouth of the first fish.

At 2:25 P.M., the phone rang. It was the Dean's office. The secretary told the student that the seminary found one tuition scholarship source which had not been tapped in years; and the seminary was able to persuade that source to support that particular student. The student went on to become the Rev. Frank Hartsell.

#10. Answered physical need: Kiwanian en route to charity function being rescued from upended car – 1990 (exact time)

We will now discuss another concrete need requiring instantaneous timeframe of fulfillment of a divine message: *exact time.*

Kiwanis International is a service organization like the Rotary, with a membership of over 333,000 in 8,450 clubs in 81 countries. The Bethesda Kiwanis Club, founded in 1944, sends some 200 underprivileged and physically handicapped children to camp for two weeks. Part of the necessary funds are raised by the annual golf outing at Bretton Woods. While a non-golfer, I participate by carrying golf bags and refreshments for the players. On the third Monday in August, 1990, I was driving along the long road to Bretton Woods with hardly another vehicle in sight. Seeing a sign, I drove into the lane to examine it. Finding that it was not where I wanted to go, I turned around to get back to the road. I felt something strange. One wheel seemed not to track. Shortly, the other back wheel also did not seem to track. I felt the back of the car tilting. Was I going to fall? "Lord, help me!" I said out loud.

Almost instantaneously, a truck appeared on the seemingly deserted road. It had gardening tools in it. The truck driver and friend rushed to my car. I asked them how I could get out. The driver said: "Oh! don't move! You are tilted over. We can't pull you out by ourselves." Immediately, another truck pulled up from the opposite side. The two in that truck also rushed to my car. The four decided to put weight on the back of the car, asking me to put the car into neutral, and slowly steer as they told me. In a few minutes, I could steer the car slowly, and inch my way out of the unsuspected deep holes right on the side of the lane into which my front wheels had sunk, upending the car, at about 35° angle!

For not one, but two trucks with gardening equipment to appear at the exact time when my car was upended, the probability is extremely miniscule. Remember that the first pair said that they could not pull me out; and instantly there came the second truck and crew. Why would they want to help a stranger? Yet they did; and drove off waving off my profuse thanks.

Prayer power profile

At Fourth Presbyterian Church in Bethesda, Maryland, we use a prayer profile (Fig. 3.1) to record identified answers to intercessory prayer, which we share publicly from time to time, in thanksgiving to the Lord.

The request

The prayer profile comprises: (1) the request, (2) the resources, and (3) the response. We saw in Chapter 1 that the intercessory prayer requests by concrete need (Fig. 1.1) make known requests for intercessory prayer at the biweekly men's prayer breakfasts.

KEY WORDS: Angel Second Class; The Highest Gift; Prayer Profile; Transcendence of Dimensions; Exact Time; Expectant Time.

Discussion Starters- Chapter 3

1. How did the visible risen Lord differ from before the crucifixion?

2. When does a divine message affirm the resurrection?

3. According to J.B. Phillips' Translation, what is the highest gift?

4. How are we a little lower than the angels?

5. When we ask the Lord to meet a concrete need in exact time, are we giving the Lord an "ultimatum?"

6. Review 6 KEY WORDS:
Angel, Second Class; The Highest Gift; Prayer Profile; Transcendence of Time; Exact Time; Expectant Time.

Complete the Prayer Power Profile for one Answered Concrete Need.

PRAYER PROFILE: Identified Answer to Prayer for Specific, Personal Need

MESSAGE DATE:
Place and Date of Identified Answer:
Place and Date of First Intercession:
Intercessee(s): Self, Family, Friend, Foe, Other

Nature of Need(s): Spiritual, Physical, Professional, Financial, Self-Realization, Mutual Realization, Other

Number of People in Need: One, Two, Three, or More
Specifics of Need(s):

Required timeframe of Effective Answer: Specific Day, Specific Week, Specific Month, 2-12 months, 1-3 years, Continuing Burden

Nature of Newly-provided Resources: Abstract, Concrete

Result of Newly-provided Resources: Acceptance of Christ, Spiritual Growth, Spiritual Maturity, Spiritual Joy, Ability to Forgive, Other
Dramatic Physical Healing, Remission of Illness, Ability to live with Disease, Ability to Grieve, Other
Receiving of Funds (Means of Funds), Obtaining of Career Placement, Obtaining Career Advancement, Receiving Professional Skills, Other
Initiation of Communications, Initiation of broken Communications, Restoration of Relationship(s), Ability to live with hard relationships, Other
OTHER (specify)

INTERCESSOR FILE
Time of Discernment of Need:

Promise claimed/Presented Need
Received Message:

Timeframe of Message: Exact Time, Expectant Time

Exact Time: "Then the father realized that this was the EXACT TIME at which Jesus had said to him, "Your son will live," (Royal official whose son was at the point of death) John 4:53 (NIV)
Expectant Time: "I will come back to you NEXT SPRING, when your wife Sarah shall have a son." Gen 18:10 (Moffatt)

Fig 3.1 Prayer Power Partnership (P3)

4

Measure of Miracles—Ancient and Modern

How do we recognize a miracle? We look at examples from the Old and the New Testaments to calibrate modern-day miracles. Each of our concrete needs is of utmost significance to us, but how does it compare with those of others who inhabit this planet, let alone with those of the inhabitants of the some 100 million other civilizations? What priority can we claim for our particular concrete need?

#11. Answered financial need: Peter's first fish providing just the 65 cents for temple tax for two – A.D. 32 (exact time)

The Psalmist exclaims: "What shall I render unto the Lord for all his benefits toward me (gifts to me)? (Psalm 116:12, KJV, NEB) He finds a way. Count: "How precious to me are your thoughts, O God! How vast is the sum of them! Were I to count them, they would outnumber the grains of sand." (Psalm 139:17-18, NIV)

Odds against Israel

One way to avoid forgetting is to remember in detail the depth of the desperation prior to the Lord's gift or benefit:

> [I]f the Lord had not been on our side
> when men attacked us,
> when their anger flared against us,
> they would have swallowed us alive
> the flood would have engulfed us,
> the torrent would have swept over us,
> the raging waters would have swept us away
> (Psalm 124: 2-5, NIV)

It is the utterly impossible odds against them that Israel had to recount in order to recognize how mighty the Lord's deliverance was. To fix ideas, let us look at the odds against the first fish that Peter would catch carrying precisely the four drachmas (65 cents).

Demand for temple tax

A year before the Last Supper, Jesus and Peter went to Capernaum.

> When they reached Capharnahum, the collectors of the half-shekel temple-tax came and asked Peter, "Does not your teacher pay the tax? He said, "Yes." Later when he went into the house Jesus anticipated what he was going to say. "What do you think, Simon?" he said. "Whom do the kings of this world get their tolls and taxes from – their own people or from aliens?" "From aliens," he said. Then Jesus said to him, "So their own people are exempt. But so that we may not offend them, go to the lake and throw out your line. Take the first fish you catch; open its mouth and you will find a five-shilling piece. Take it and give it to them for my tax and yours." (Matthew 17:24-27, RSV, MOF, PHI, NIV)

The lake

Jesus told Peter to "go to the lake." Capernaum is situated on the shore of the Sea of Galilee, which is also known as Lake Gennesaret. The lake is really River Jordan rising on Mount Hermon to form the lake. And the river continues its north-to-south journey, dividing the 250-meter Palestine into two.The fish could come from anywhere in River Jordan, namely, from anywhere along the 250-kilometer length. The Jordan might accommodate one million fish.

The fish

"Patros Fish," or "Peter's Fish" is a tourist attraction in today's Galilee. After a swim in the clear blue waters of the calm lake, one is ready to taste the nine- to ten- inch cooked fish served uncut on a platter. Another way of looking at it is to say that Jordan is one million fish-lengths long. We could divide the whole river into vertical imaginary fish-lengths. Further, the fish can be in any of the thousands of horizontal fish-widths across the Jordan. But we will drastically simplify by stipulating that the fish can be only in each discrete (separate) vertical fish-lengths. The one million fish can be in any of the one million fish-lengths, making the probability of one particular fish being in one particular fish-length: 1 in 1 trillion.

The time

Jesus did not tell Peter when or where he should cast his rod. What is the probability of one fish being at a particular fish-length at a particular second in one of the 86,400 seconds in a day? It is roughly 1 in 100,000 trillion.

The first fish

Notice that Jesus told Peter: "Take the first fish you catch." Any one of the fish in any one of the fish-lengths could qualify as the "first fish" because Peter could cast his rod nearly anywhere at any time. Even if we assume that not 1, but 100, fish are caught on the fly at one time, there are some 1,000 trillion candidate fish that could carry the four drachmas.

Notice that the fish should hold exactly 65 cents: no more, no less. Of course, if every fish carried exactly 65 cents, then word would get around, and there would have been a "fish rush" that would put the "gold rush" to shame. None is recorded; so we must conclude that there was only a single fish which carried the 65 cents. If only one fish carried the 65 cents, all the other fish in the fish-lengths in Jordan did not carry the money. Peter could have caught any one of the (1,000 trillion-1) fish that did not carry the required 65 cents In other words, the odds against Peter's need being met were about 1,000 trillion to 1.

The audacity of faith

When we pray for specific, personal needs, often time-sensitive needs, we are expecting the particular grain of sand representing our special need to be picked up out of all the trillions of grains of sand of our planet.

Peter's time-sensitive need

Peter needed 32½ cents to pay his temple tax; and another 32½ cents for Jesus, and he needed it immediately. The chances of his not getting the 65 cents at any time were stupendous; and his not getting it when he needed it, and not getting it from the first fish that he caught from somewhere in Jordan at some unspecified time, were astronomical. We define *miracle:* An occurrence with odds 1 billion to 1 against it. The odds against Peter's need being met were about 1,000 trillion to 1.

Resources to meet concrete needs

It is only the faith in the utmost significance dares us to look to the author of every good and perfect gift for our specific needs – needs which require specific, concrete resources. We can recognize three categories of resources: (1) recompensing resources, (ii) recurrent resources, and (iii) renewing resources.

Resource categories: (1) Recompensing resources
Peter needed to pay off an exact obligation: 32½ cents for temple-tax for himself and 32½ cents for Jesus. The seminary student (#9. Answered Financial Need in chapter 2) needed to pay off an exact obligation – the tuition for the semester. Such obligations require resources to recompense the obligation, or *recompensing resources.*

Resource categories: (2) Recurring resources
While Peter's need was a one-time need, Elijah's was a recurring need – occurring morning and evening.

#12. Answered physical need: Elijah being fed twice daily for about two years – B.C. 929 (expectant time)

The bold prophet of the Lord, Elijah, faced the king of Israel, Ahab, and told him: "As the LORD. the God of Israel, lives, whom I serve, there will be neither dew nor rain in the next few years except at my word." (1 Kings 17:1, NIV)

To a country dependent on agriculture, absence of rain is one of the worst pieces of news. And the heavens were going to be shut until this prophet alone reopened them! Elijah would win no popularity contest in the court of Israel! He had to flee for his life. And he was sent to the Kerith Ravine, east of the Jordan. He was to be fed with bread and meat by the ravens – which are carnivorous animals. In other words, a raven kills its prey to feed itself; and that very meat is brought by it to feed Elijah: "You will drink from the brook, and I have ordered the ravens to feed you there."... The ravens brought him bread and meat in the morning, and bread and meat in the evening, and he drank from the brook. (1 Kings 17: 4,6, NIV)

Each morning, at least two ravens had to bring Elijah his breakfast. If one in a thousand ravens would abandon all its natural inclinations, and bring meat, not to its own nest, but to a bearded animal of another species, that would be a miracle. But not one, but two ravens had to work together to bring the man the breakfast. If the bread-bringing raven is as rare as the meat-bringing raven, then the two appearing together is an event which can occur 1 in one million times. That is only one breakfast. Ravens providing breakfast and dinner have a chance of 1 in million times million – just for 1 day!

If he hid by the brook for half the drought, Elijah was fed morning and evening for more than five hundred days. The chance of Elijah receiving his breakfast and dinner for two days in a row is million times million raised to the power of 2; for 3 days, million million raised to the power of 3, ..., for 500 days, it is million times million raised to the 500th power! The resources required to meet recurring needs of breakfast and dinner are recurring resources.

Resource categories: (3) Renewing resources

When the brook runs dry, Elijah is ordered to go to Zarephath in Sidon.

#13. Answered physical need: Elijah being fed at home for about a year and a half – B.C. 927 (expectant time)

Jesus makes a point of the fact that none of the widows in Israel was chosen to host Elijah: "I assure you that there were many widows in Israel in Elijah's time... Yet Elijah was not sent to any of them, but to a widow in Zarephath in the region of Sidon." (Luke 4:25-26, NIV)

The widows of Israel are mentioned because they would indeed be considered logical candidates to host Elijah. Adding the number of widows in Sidon, there would probably be conservatively some 10,000 widows who could host Elijah. Finding the one widow has a chance of 1 in ten thousand. However, what were the chances of her being able to provide for Elijah for 1½ to 2 years? As a widow, who would have been recognized by her black dress, she was quite probably without any visible means of support. The fact that she was collecting kindling wood at the city gate, which is public domain, means that she would be on what we call welfare rolls, if there were such rolls available.

Elijah requests a drink of water, something very scarce after some 18 months of drought. And he asks for a cake of bread. But that cake of bread is half of her worldly possessions: she is gathering the few sticks to take home "and make a meal for myself and my son, that we may eat it – and die." If the probability of Elijah getting a single cake of bread from the widow is 1 in ten thousand, the chance of his getting another cake of bread is zero! Yet, that was the hostess to whom Elijah was sent for some five hundred days. If the widow were not on her last meal, the chance of Elijah being fed one meal a day for five hundred successive days would be 1 in ten thousand raised to the 500th power (1 in a billion is 1 in ten thousand raised to the 2.25th power)

How is Elijah going to be fed? Through renewing resources: "For this is what the LORD, the God of Israel, says: The jar of flour will not be used up and the jug of oil will not run dry until the day the LORD gives rain on the land." (1 Kings 17:14, NIV) The renewing resources met the needs of Elijah, the widow of Zarephath and her son.

To be granted the resources to meet a concrete need, it must first be considered. While our own need of the moment seems most pressing, let us consider the odds against it being even considered!

Odds against our concrete need being considered by God

If the five billion people on earth each has a concrete need once a year, that totals five billion needs. One concrete need a day raises the number to 1,825 billion a year. One concrete need an hour produces 43,800 billion concrete needs a year. Each need is specific; each requires recompensing, recurring or renewing resources.

If the earth were the only planet, the nearly 44 trillion needs a year is a conservative number. But our earth is only one of 9 planets which revolve around the sun. The sun is only a medium-size star. Each star can support several planets as our sun does; and some could support many more.

Which concrete needs get granted?

Does it make any difference whether there are 20 zeros or 200 zeros in the number of concrete needs? After all, I just want one tiny need of mine to be met right now!

That is precisely the point. Imagine that you are standing on the beach. There are millions and millions of grains of sand as far as the eye can see, and well beyond, stretching far, far into the unseen. Your particular concrete need is a single grain of sand. Granting your particular need means picking up that single, solitary grain of sand, called A.

It is a big beach. If you can stand on the beach, so can your neighbor. It is quite possible that he too has a concrete need: another grain of sand. He too earnestly wishes that his need will be granted: that grain of sand picked out be the other single, solitary grain of sand, called B.

Which should be picked – A or B? Remember that it is not A or B alone that enters the picture. All the other grains of sand on the endless stretch of beach vie for the honor.

The chance of picking A is not one in two, or one in 100 (1 with 2 zeros), one in 1,000 (1 with 3 zeros), but more like one in 1 with 20 or more zeros! Once picked, if the chance of it being met is that of Peter getting 65 cents from the first fish he caught (1 in 100,000 trillion —1 in 1 with 18 zeros), the odds against your concrete need being met are 1 with 38 zeros to 1, or 1 in 100 trillion times trillion times trillion.

From utmost insignificance to utmost significance

The utterly insignificant need of mine in the scheme of the concrete needs of five billion people is transformed into one of utmost significance. That transformation is a gift: gift from the Infinite God who is the Lord of the Universe. It is God who picks up that single, solitary grain of sand that is my pressing concrete need of the moment, and grants it ample resources.

Definition of intercession

We find that God chooses to answer intercessions by one (Abram) in behalf of another (Abimelech), requiring a new community to be formed with each intercession of the intercessor and the intercessee. Since society is two or more interacting persons, and since personality is self-expression in society, we see that intercession is a means of grace in society. Because the Christian community is a sanctified society, and because it is the Christian community which has the means of grace of intercession available to them, it is proper to say that

> Intercession is the setting apart of one person(s) for other(s) to transmit God's restoring of relationship(s) and / or providing of resources for specific situations. (George K. Chacko, *Interceding with the Infinite: Practicing Prayer Power,* Leadership Ministries International, Bethesda, Md., 1985, p.182.)

The specific resources depend on the purposes. Therefore, the means can be abstract or concrete. Again, the needs may be personal, relating to a single person; or the needs may be group needs, pertaining to two or more persons. We can define identified answer as

> The pinpointing of abstract and / or concrete resources which are adequate and appropriate to accomplish personal, interpersonal, and / or collective instances of concurrence between what-ought-to- be and what is. (*Ibid.*, p.13)

KEY WORDS/PHRASES: Intercession; Identified Answer

Discussion Starters – Chapter 4

1. Differentiate between the type of resources Elijah received by the brook and in Zarephath.

2. Show why Peter's first fish carrying precisely 65 cents is a miracle.

3. Discuss how your concrete need is miraculously considered by God.

4. Sketch how the ravens feeding Elijah is a miracle.

5. KEY WORDS/ PHRASES: Define "Intercession," "Identified Answer."

5

Reality of Resurrection in Prayer Power

Most people are uncomfortable with death. They would rather not think about it, secretly hoping that thereby it would go away. Shakespeare's Hamlet prefers the here for fear of the hereafter:

For who would bear the whips and scorns of time…
But that the dread of something after death,
The undiscover'd country from whose bourn
No traveler returns, puzzles the will
And makes us rather bear the ills we have
Than fly to others that we know not of?
Thus conscience does make cowards of us all
(*Hamlet*, Act III, Scene I)

In contrast, the Christian faith is founded on resurrection: A Traveler who returned on the third day as promised, from the very bourn [boundary] of the undiscover'd country.

The fundamental fact of resurrection is the transcending of dimensions – from the finite to the infinite. It is the reality of resurrection that imparts power to prayer. Can we know our own death ahead of time? Can we preside over it when the time comes? Can we transcend time and space to communicate with those whom we have left behind on earth? Read Answered Spiritual Needs #14, 17; and Answered Physical Needs #15, 26. These Christian experiences are presented in the context of contemporary concerns.

Death and taxes

In 1789, Benjamin Franklin reflected on the new U.S. Constitution and its prospects for survival. "Our Constitution is in actual operation; everything appears to promise that it will last, but in this world nothing is certain but death and taxes." (Benjamin Franklin, Letter to M. Leroy 1789, in *Bartlett's Familiar Quotations*, Little, Brown, Boston, 14th edition, 1968,

p. 423) Taxes presuppose taxable wealth, a luxury unknown to billions of inhabitants of this planet, leaving death as the only universal certainty everyone has to face. The Chinese view death as a passage into another world requiring provisions complete with paper money, while the Hindus, comprising 83 percent of India's 850-million population view it as the release of the eternal *atman* imprisoned in the human body.

"Fellow traveler"

Mark Twain, in his story "Fellow Traveler," describes his encounter on a lonely train late at night with a ticketless traveler who was waking him up quite rudely every time he dozed off. He tried appealing to the civic sense of the intruder, tried pointing out the illegality of his action, and even threatened to call the police – but all to no avail. He tried attacking the intruder, flaying his arms, but the latter was too swift for Twain; he would move out of Twain's reach.

Resigned to his plight, Twain contemplated the flight of the intruder as finally the offending mosquito flew off into the night. We are all like the mosquito, mused Mark Twain, coming in from the dark, fluttering around the light for a little while, and going out into the dark again.

Gallup polls on the hereafter

Mark Twain's view of our going out into the dark would be contradicted by 7 out of 10 Americans.; and more interestingly, by 75 percent of the young people. Says Dr. Gallup:

> We've surveyed a national sample of the American people to ascertain the details of their beliefs and attitudes toward life after death. One consistent, overwhelming belief that pervades our studies and that probably has been a commonly held assumption by most humans since prehistoric times is that heaven does, indeed, exist.

At the Gallup Poll, we've asked national audiences in 1952, 1965 and 1980 this question: "Do you think there is a Heaven, where people who have led good lives are eternally rewarded?"

A consistent seven out of ten people have responded "yes," and there is every reason to believe that the number would have been at least as high in earlier years, when religious faith was more pervasive....

You might think that the older you get, the more likely you are to begin to think about – and believe in – the pearly gates. But actually, we've found that the highest response for belief in heaven-more than 75 percent-came from young people from 18 to 24 years of age. (George Gallup, Jr., *Adventures in Immortality*, McGraw-Hill, New York, 1982, pp. 58-9)

#14. Answered spiritual need: Precognition of one's own death and presiding over it – 1974; 1977 (expectant time)

What does it mean when a Christian says: "I see my chariot approaching?"

Maternal Grandfather Matthew predicting his death three years in advance

When I went back to India from the States in 1974 with wife Yo, son Rajah and daughter Ashia, my maternal grandfather Matthew was 94. Yo said in typical Chinese fashion: "We will come back to celebrate your 100th birthday." He waved it off. Later when I was alone with him in his bedroom, he said: "I will be around for two to three years." He died in 2¾ years.

Calling back daughters returning to their homes

He had a lingering cold for about a month. Both my mother's surviving younger sisters had arrived in Mallappally, Kerala, one from Bombay (1,200 miles) and another from Ernakulam (75 miles) to visit him. Seeing that he was improving, they decided to return to their homes. They would first go to the younger aunt's home (4 hours' journey), and then the older aunt would fly to Bombay (8-9 hours' journey including to and from airport).

There is no telephone in grandfather Matthew's house. There is one phone in the village, to reach which you have to walk more than a mile. You have to book a call, wait for an hour or so, depending on the distance, and when the trunk line and feeder lines are clear, you will be called to pick up a phone in a booth – at least a 2-hour operation. After spending the time, the call may not be completed if the party is not at home. Try again!

Grandfather's decision to call his daughters back was not taken lightly. He well knew the great difficulties of just reaching his daughters. Had he known earlier, he could have easily asked them to stay on for another day or two. The fact that he didn't means that he didn't know any different. Now he wanted urgently to reach them, and have them come back. He also asked for his minister. The minister had already called on him a few days earlier and prayed with him. But now grandfather wanted him to give him last rites. Since grandfather was by no means an alarmist, his instructions were not discounted, but promptly carried out.

Saying goodbye

By phone, they reached the younger daughter's home, where the older daughter was getting ready for her flight the next day. Hearing the news, the husband of the younger daughter went back with daughters to Mallappally. After his daughters returned, grandfather asked everyone to assemble in the living room. He looked up from his favorite chair, and talked to each one, asking after each member of their families with full alertness and recall. After talking to everyone, he said, "Stand back, I want to see each of you one more time." After he held each in his vision, he said: "Let us pray."

"I see my chariot approaching"

After praying, he looked at the assembled, and said, "I am going to sleep now. I don't want you to cry." He lifted his eyes up and said, "I see my chariot approaching." He sat back and died peacefully.

Consciously announcing a well recognized religious symbol

Did grandfather actually see a chariot approaching? A physical verification is impossible. No infrared or ultra-violet photograph was taken at the moment of the approaching chariot. But there is no doubt that grandfather saw it as well as the people he was talking to just moments earlier. In the New Testament, a physician reports on a dying declaration:

> Stephen, filled through all his being with the Holy Spirit, looked steadily up into Heaven. He saw the glory of God, and Jesus himself standing at his right hand. "Look!" he exclaimed, "there is a rift in the sky;I can see the Son of Man standing at God's right hand!" (Acts 7:55-56, PHI, NEB)

"The Son of Man standing at God's right hand" was certainly not a universally recognized symbol. On the contrary, Stephen's reported sighting of Jesus, whom the Jews had crucified only two months ago, so infuriated his immediate listeners that they refused to listen to the damning blasphemy, and hurried to put him to death by a most painful means:

> At this they gave a great shout and put their fingers in their ears. Yelling with fury, as one man they made a rush at him and hustled him out of the city and stoned him. (Acts 7: 57-58, NEB, PHI)

The vehemence of the reaction of the listeners attests to the fact that they heard Stephen, and they understood him. They did not say: "He is babbling," and "Let us ignore him." On the contrary, what he said was very real to the listeners. They did not question it at all, but acted upon it.

I doubt that psychoanalyst Carl Jung would consider Stephen to be dreaming. Even if it were a dream, Jung would consider it a fact and consider it within the Christian context: "I take dreams as facts that are invaluable for diagnosis.... [I]n the case of a devout Christian, the symbol of the cross can be interpreted only in its Christian context." So, Stephen's vision has to be understood within the context of what he so firmly believed in that he was actually being martyred for it.

Elisha's witnessing Elijah's ascension

While I recognized what grandfather meant by the approaching chariot, I searched the Scriptures to discover the precise context and content. The closest Biblical narrative is that of Elisha, the hand-picked successor to Elijah, the great prophet of Israel. Elijah asks Elisha: "Tell me, what can I do for you before I am taken from you?" Elisha replies: "Let me inherit a double portion of your spirit." (2 Kings 2:9, NIV) He could have his wish only on one condition:

> [I]f you see me when I am taken from you, it shall be yours, but not if you fail to see me. Suddenly, as they walked and talked, a chariot of fire with horses of fire drove between them, and Elijah went up by a whirlwind into heaven . When Elisha saw this he cried, out, "My father, my father! The chariots and horsemen of Israel!" And Elisha saw him no more. (2 Kings 2:9-12, MOF, NIV)

All those who heard grandfather had no question as to what was meant by the chariot approaching. The instantly-recognized phrase meant that grandfather was going to heaven even as Elijah did.

Widely shared cultural symbolism of the chariot

I wondered if there were a shared cultural tradition about the chariot. I had seen wooden chariots in my boyhood in my father's village at the annual Hindu festival. The graven image of the god would be set high inside the chariot which was gaily decorated. There were no horses, however. In fact, the wheels of the chariot were hardly smooth. Men would heave and pull the chariot with great vigor from the temple once around the open field in front, by the banks of the river. That was not the chariot any of grandfather's listeners visualized. Was the chariot a symbol to the Christians – something which pointed beyond itself?

Time, the Chariot

As I pondered, the words of a hymn I have sung as a boy came to my mind. I was twelve when my father's mother died. I recalled the extended family being gathered in the large hall where my paternal grandmother was lying on the mat made of hemp on the bed made of woven rope. Most people slept on the floor, spreading a mat and rolling up towels for a pillow. So, the bed and the real pillow were a luxury. The wife of my father's oldest brother was sitting on the floor behind my grandmother's headrest. My mother later said that my grandmother waved her right hand, as though saying that she was leaving. I remember that the wife of my father's oldest brother was the first one to cry out and kiss my departed grandmother's forehead. Later, I saw my father crying and kissing the cheeks of my grandmother who had just died. I recall everyone crying, grown-ups and children alike, with no effort on anyone's part to keep a stiff upper lip, or to deny that death had taken place.

In the village, where we do not have funeral parlors and directors, the village carpenter (a Hindu) arrives to make a plain coffin of pinewood. I remember our buying black glossy paper to paste on all sides of the coffin, and gold paper to use as borders. The coffin was papered with rice-paste. It must have been a great catharsis to spend hours decorating the coffin which would carry our grandmother on her final journey. The coffin is carried on the shoulders of village people to the church, about half a mile away. I recall the long procession of relatives and friends which followed the coffin, singing the traditional hymn of burial:

> Time the Chariot, on Time the Chariot
> Heavenly journey do I make;
> Hastening to see my own homeland,
> Running fast there to arrive.

Thus, we find that the chariot is time itself. Heaven is the homeland toward which the Christian is racing all his life: "Our citizenship is in heaven. And we eagerly await a Savior from there, the Lord Jesus Christ." (Ephesians 3:20, NIV)

Precognition transcending time and space

Finite man is bound by space and time. We can be only at one place at one time. We cannot say, be giving a lecture in Hong Kong while watching in Moscow, a live Bolshoi Ballet performance.

Divine delimitation: infinite God as a human in finite time and Space

God, the Infinite, by definition, is not so limited. However, the God who is not limited by time or space or other dimensions, cannot communicate with man, the finite, simply because infinite begins where the finite ends.

> Finite man cannot comprehend the Infinite God, even as the tiny electric bulb in the living room cannot tap directly into the avalanche of electric power at the power plant. Further, God's dimensions themselves are infinite, which means that there is no conceivable way of finite man communicating with even a single dimension, let alone the infinity of dimensions.
>
> So the Infinite God must take the initiative to communicate with finite man-which requires a *Dimensional Transform*. That Transform must communicate to man in a language that man understands. Since there are hundreds of languages, the language must be valid across time and space, across geographic boundaries and from age to age.
>
> Since the communication is to man, it only stands to reason that anyone other than a man could not communicate directly to man. A being with more dimensions than man would be beyond man; a being with less dimensions than man would be beneath man. Neither would be able to communicate man-to-man. Therefore , the Dimensional Transform *must reveal Infinite God as finite man*: finite in time and space; finite in geography, in culture; in language; in work, etc. Yet, the communication must be that of the Infinite God....
>
> We cannot understand God's creation of man without His permitting man to depart from the ideal (what-can-be): Which departure is the Cross. *The Cross is Eternal, so long as man can choose to make what-is different from what-can-be.* The Eternal Cross was historically revealed on Calvary. If Christ's Historic Cross communicates God's Eternal Cross, Christ is God (emphasis added) . (George K. Chacko, *Interceding with the Infinite: Practicing Prayer Power*, Leadership International, Bethesda, Md., 1985, pp. 77, 82.)

Thus we see that even as a transformer is needed to step the electric current of massive power down to the voltage that can be transmitted through the electric power lines into the homes to light the 60-watt light bulbs, so also the Infinite God must use a Dimensional Transform to communicate His reason for creation, namely His love of mankind, delimiting the Infinite by the finite dimensions of time and space. Unless man is created a robot, he is free not to choose the ideal, or what-can-be.

Whoever can communicate to a person the love of God that wants what-can-be for mankind, must be God. Recall how Solomon found out the true mother when he ordered a sword to cut into two the living baby whom two women claimed as their child. One woman agreed, saying that if she could not have the baby, neither could the other. But the true mother implored the king not to kill the living baby, even if she could not have him. Solomon declared that the woman who was willing even to give up the baby instead of having him killed, showed the mother's heart. So also, whoever can disclose the eternal cross in God's heart can only be God in human form: Jesus Christ.

Power – Here and hereafter

Christ's resurrection is the source and sustainer of the power of prayer. Paul is most eloquent about how prayer is empowered by the resurrection power.

His thesis in the following Ephesian passage, made clearer by splicing different translations of the Bible, is that the tremendous power available to us (Prayer Power) is the same mighty power which raised Christ from the dead (Resurrection Power):

> Ever since I heard about your faith in the Lord Jesus
> and your love for all the saints
> I never cease to give thanks for you and
> I never give up praying for you; and this is my prayer:
> That the God of our Lord Jesus Christ, the all-glorious Father,
> will give you spiritual wisdom and the insight to know more of him;
> that you may receive that inner illumination of the spirit which will make you realize
> how great is the hope to which he is calling you—
> the significance and splendor of the inheritance
> promised to Christians – and how tremendous is the power available to us who believe in God.
> That power is the same mighty power which he exerted in raising Christ from the dead
> and seating him at his right hand in the heavenly sphere
> above all the angelic Rulers, Authorities, Powers, and Lords,
> above every Name that could ever be used
> not only in this world but also in the world to come
> (Ephesians 1:15-21, NIV, MOF, PHI, KJV)

God lifting the veil of time

We said in Chapter 3, that as finite beings, we do not know what will happen the very next moment. However, God is infinite, which means to Him, Yesterday = Today = Tomorrow. When Mr. A on the East Coast of the United States calls at 11 P.M. Monday, then Mr. B in Hong Kong receives the call at 11 A.M. Tuesday. But to someone looking down at both the U.S. and Hong Kong from a geosynchronous satellite 22,500 miles up, Monday = Tuesday. To us, tomorrow is unseen, and unseeable; but it is known to God. And if He chooses to lift the veil of time, and show us what is going to occur tomorrow, nine months hence, 2¾ years hence, that message lets us transcend time and space either in the immediate (exact time) or eventually (expectant time). We will now look at two instances in which God lifted the veil of time.

#15. Answered physical need: Precognition of one more year of life for a dying individual – 1982 (expectant time)

On my way back from India in August 1982, I stopped in Taipei where I hoped to go on a Fulbright Professorship in 1983. After Sunday lunch with pastor Mike VanderPol and surgeon Dr. Sam Noordhoff, we discussed what I could do next year.

Several months earlier, Sam was suddenly stricken with a neurological disease not yet named, which had no known cure. A brilliant Canadian neurologist in Taipei diagnosed the disease to be similar to what his own mother died from within six months after its discovery. As we were discussing 1983, Sam said gravely:"I don't know if I will be around." No sooner did Sam say those words than I felt apprehended to look him fully in the face, and say: "You certainly will be." That was the Lord's guaranteeing one year of life to a dying man, transcending time. The message would be fulfilled in expectant time.

Back home, I had no word from or about Sam, but prayed for him frequently. Six months later, after my morning prayer, I told Yo: "Sam is much better." Six months later, we learned in Taipei that it was indeed the exact time when Sam began to recover. The certain knowledge of Sam's recovery half way around the world transcended space, even as the certain knowledge of his one year survival transcended time. The expectant time of Sam's survival, and the exact time of the start of his recovery are gifts permitting us to peek behind the veil of time.

#16. Answered physical need: Precognition of bedridden cancer patient travelling abroad – 1983

A second instance relates to Dr. Cliff Robinson, Founder of Leadership Ministries International (LMI), who succeeded in getting legislators and executives in government and industry in countries throughout the world to meet on a regular basis for prayer. Yo and I were at the opening of the new LMI offices on the first Friday in December,1981. As we left the celebrations we all urged Cliff to have his persistent backache examined. The next week he did. The backache was from cancer! A most virulent form of cancer was raging through his bone. The doctors were baffled by the virulence.

> In August, 1983, I was in Seoul, teaching U.S. military officers working for the Master of Science Degree of the University of Southern California, where I am Professor of Systems Science. During the 11 o'clock worship service on Sunday, August 21, I was led to dedicate my solo broadcast of Mallotte's "Lord's Prayer" to Cliff, who, when stuck by virulent cancer 20 months ago, prayed cheerfully: "Thy will be done!" As I prepared for the solo, I was seized of an exciting, incredible message, which I sent to Cliff: "Do you believe that you will stand in Korea next year?" I could hardly believe it, because in monthly LMI updates, Cliff was reported as making welcome, but slow, progress. The LMI Update seven months later published a tentative itinerary , beginning with April 13 departure from Washington, D.C., and arrival in Korea for the National Prayer Breakfast Meetings beginning April 29!
>
> The Message I transmitted apparently came at a time of deep sense of helplessness with respect to recovery. Getting around the house, let alone getting around town, was a major chore. Extremely painful shingles plagued Cliff for quite some time. To suggest that he could resume local prayer breakfasts would have been a far distant goal. When domestic travel itself was too unrealistic a dream, the certain assurance of international travel was truly astounding! Later Cliff said when he received the message we [he and wife Betty] wept!" (Chacko, *Interceding with the Infinite*, p. 31)

#17. Answered spiritual need: Bright-raimented Robinson conveying in Seoul his passage to glory just as the cable on his death reached Taipei – 1985 (exact time)

Cliff was delighted to have been able to make the international trip, particularly his visit to India where he served for 18 years as missionary.

But the trip was too much for him, and he had to cut it short and return home. Yo and I had called on him when we came home during Christmas, 1984, and Cliff was ambulatory, and able to drive into town for prayer breakfasts. The pastor of Fourth Presbyterian Church in Bethesda, where Cliff and Betty worshiped, had recently flown to the bedside of his favorite dying aunt. When I expressed condolences after Sunday worship service, Rev. Dr. Robert Norris said with great assurance: "She's in glory!" That was the only time I had heard the expression. Its significance will soon become apparent.

Returning to Taipei, Yo worked furiously on her cookbook, with dawn-to-dusk photo sessions on each of her recipes. I went on ahead to Seoul to teach USC students in May. I was teaching the most mathematical of our courses: Deterministic Models in Decision-Making. I had no recent news of Cliff's condition, and no idea of what was happening. After teaching my class on Yongsan Army Base, I was mentally working out the proof for some result. My letter to Betty Robinson dated June 5, 1985 says:

> Dear Betty:
> Yo called me from Taipei when she received your cable about Cliff's going into glory. An hour before her call I was walking home from my class at Yongsan Army Base, and suddenly heard myself say: "Goodbye Cliff, I'll meet you in glory. Praise God for the Resurrection!", and I remember seeing Cliff's big smile from above. Every time I think of Cliff, it is that smiling face, full of life and joy, that comes to mind. His passing into glory had made resurrection a fact of life, and continue to minister to me. Praise the Lord!

I still vividly recall the appearance, as I was walking home, of Cliff to my left in a dazzling white jacket. Only his bust was visible, but his face was ruddy and smile bright, as in 1979 when we had gone to Russia on his World Family Friendship Tour, two years before his cancer. Was the radiant raiment a culturally-shared symbol? Luke says that when the women brought to Jesus' sepulcher the spices they had prepared, they found the stone rolled away, and Jesus' body missing:

> "Behold two men stood by them in shining garments (KJV), or Two men flashed on them dazzling raiment (Moffatt), or Two men in clothes that gleamed like lightning stood beside them (NIV),or Two men suddenly stood at their elbow, dressed in dazzling light (Phillips)." (Luke 24:4)

Clearly, the dazzling white jacket points to angels: Cliff as an angel. Concentrating as I was on a mathematical proof, and not thinking about Cliff on my way home in Seoul, the sudden intrusion into my peripheral vision of a physically-transformed Cliff donned in a dazzling white jacket never seen before, precisely at the time the cable about his death reached my wife in Taipei, is another peek behind the veil of time. I would not hear of Cliff's death for another hour when my wife would call me in Seoul from Taipei; we had no inkling that death was near at all. Cliff's appearance transcended time and space: in Korea at the exact time the cable on Cliff's death was recorded in Taipei.

God's angels – Here and hereafter

In 1989, just before I left Taipei, Tom Dedricks, editor of *Chimes,* Taipei International Church Newsletter, asked me to write a short article on Angels, which I will excerpt below. Five years earlier, at a Tuesday prayer breakfast meeting, the Rev. Mike VanderPol had asked the question: Does anybody know much about angels? I discussed it at briefly in my 1985 book on intercessory prayer. Angels transcend time and space, two dimensions which limit finite man. What does such transcendence mean? What do we know from the Scripture?

Billy Graham at National Presbyterian Church, Washington, D.C.

Billy Graham came down to the choir room with our minister Louis Evans, to pray with us before the 11 o'clock worship. After prayer, he said to the minister: "Louie, when we get to heaven, your work and mine will be finished, but (pointing to us in the choir) their work would have just begun!

Singing for ever, strumming heavenly harps, is the full-time job traditionally associated with winged angels in flowing robes. Pardon me, but I think the job description is at best partial.

Messenger – beyond time

Angel means messenger. We ar familiar with the angel announcing Issac to Abraham, John to Zacharias, and Jesus to Mary. All the three instances are interventionist – God entering human history. Sorry about the big word, but that sets Christianity apart from the religions around us in Taiwan, which are immanent religions wherein there is no creation, but a cycle of birth and death of the earth and everything and everybody in it.

From Second to First Class

Look around you-both in time and space. Did God send you a message about an event or relationship in the future? The one who brought it to you had no wings, but what he said or did sustained you at a critical time. That was an Angel, Second Class. Like the bystander on whom, the new sheriff pins a badge and says: "You are now a Deputy," ASCs are deputized for specific messages. If trustworthy in small messages, they get to communicate bigger ones.

Intervening across Dimensions

Mortals are bound by time. We can be only in one place at one time. To die means to be beyond time-beyond the limitation of time. We can then be simultaneously in Taipei, Paris, and New York; on Jupiter, Mars, and Moon.

To do what? Luke (22:43) tells us that at the hour of Jesus' agony, an angel appeared to strengthen him (not sing to him). When our struggle is fierce, and our future forlorn, an angel is dispatched with the message simultaneously to the specific needs of several people in several places: "Look, see how your special need is already met tomorrow!" What a privilege to look forward to!

KEY WORD: Precognition.

Discussion Starters – Chapter 5

1.What does it mean when a Christian says: "I see my chariot approaching?"

2. Discuss precognition as empowerment by resurrection power with respect to: (1) certainty of life for another year of a dying man; (2) travel abroad seven months later by a bedridden cancer patient.

3. Discuss the most important feature of angelic life.

4. Review 1 KEY WORD: Precognition.
Prayerfully share precognition granted you on a verified event.

6

Recompensing Resources For Exact Time I

Thankfully recognizing that it is the Infinite God alone Who elevates to utmost significance our relatively insignificant needs, we recount different types of concrete needs, which require different types of resources.

Exact time

The Lord's answers in exact time is recalled with respect to two professional needs in Chapter 6, and with respect to one each of financial, physical, relational, and spiritual needs in Chapter 7.

#18. Answered professional need: Hostile superior blocking "Joe's" promotion dramatically reversed – 1986 (exact time)

In September 1986 I was teaching an adult Sunday school class at Fourth Presbyterian Church, using as the text my book *Interceding with the Infinite: Practicing Prayer Power*. At the end of the second Sunday of the class, a foreign-born member, evidently under great strain, came to me and said with considerable agitation. "I am at the end of my tether. I beg you to pray for me." We will call him "Joe."

Extreme criticality of timeframe of required resources

Joe spoke of an "impossible boss" who has had been pushing him into one impossible corner after another. Seeking to escape the "hell" of working under the particular boss, Joe had sought a reassignment. A suitable opening in the Paris office of his company led to him being offered the position.

The Paris office wanted Joe and family to be in place by a specific date, which was then less than a month away. He needed the annual leave due him to wind up his affairs, rent his house, pack, and move. However, his boss was bent on not letting Joe use the annual leave due him. If Joe could not get his leave, he would not be able to carry out the very many chores essential for the move.

Paris could not wait for even a single day. No sooner would Joe report to the Paris office than he would be sent to Norway on assignment. The one person who would have to brief Joe on the assignment was scheduled to leave the day after Joe's scheduled arrival in Norway.

The boss was effectively vetoing Joe's 3-year assignment, which had cost him several months of hard and persistent work. Joe did not want the Paris office to know the stumbling blocks thrown by his boss. I asked, "Could the personnel office intervene?" Joe could speak to the personnel office the following day, but he had little hope of that office being able to change the mind of his boss. "I am really at the end of my tether. Tomorrow is going to be the hardest day I've ever had. I beg you, please pray for me."

Discerning the need

As I listened to Joe, I felt led to intercede for him. So I told him: "You don't have to beg me to pray for you. I would be happy to do that for you."

While I had seen Joe and his wife in the Interceding class, I did not know his name or phone number. The class met in four separate groups, and discussed the assigned chapters for the day. I would eavesdrop on each group during the discussion, so that when all the four groups assembled at the end of the hour, I could address specific concerns that the different groups had raised.

Message about a future event

Immediately after the class, I had to rush off to several appointments, so that it was only late at night that I could intercede for the nameless individual in the Interceding class. The next morning as I again interceded for him, I felt strongly an unexpected, time-sensitive message: "Ask him what happened at 9:45 this morning."

I had prayed at about 8:15 a.m. Notice that the message specifies something significant happening 1 hour and 30 minutes later.

Gideon's rule

How do I know if the "9:45 A.M. event" is not simply my own wishful thinking? I apply "Gideon's rule" to the perceived answer. This three-pronged test of Gideon ensured that he was indeed listening to God, and not to his own wishful thinking.

Applying Gideon's rule to the future event

To guard against hearing what I want to hear, instead of what God wants me to hear, I apply Gideon's rule to identified answers to intercessory prayer.

Does the identical message recur unbidden three times?

After receiving the message that a significant, positive, development would occur in precisely 90 minutes, I spent an intense day at the office. At at least two other times, the message about the 9:45 A.M. occurrence in Joe's situation came up in identical form, entirely unbidden "like a bolt out of the blue," when I was not thinking about Joe.

Still, I held off from finding out Joe's phone number to ask him if anything special happened on Monday at 9:45 lest it might influence his reply. By Tuesday evening, I was permitted to try to reach Joe. But could not get his number, which was not helped by my not knowing his name.

"A miracle happened last week"

It was not until the following Sunday that I saw Joe again. Just as I was about to make my summary remarks to the Interceding class, he came up to me. In place of the grave, downcast man of the previous Sunday, weighed down with the weight of the world on his shoulders, there was a beaming man who said, "A miracle happened last week...." "Yes, I know," I interrupted, "Monday at 9:45 A.M.."

His closest friend said later, "I saw his jaw drop. I have never seen him do that, ever. You know he is quite reserved and proper." The friend gestured a space of six inches, saying, "His jaw dropped like this."

I had to move on to start the summary session, without being able to discuss what the miracle was. Even if something wonderful happened, why would anyone note the time?

Joe said, "Last Monday was going to be the worst day of my life. I was at the end of my tether. I looked at the watch at 9:37 or 9:38 because I saw my boss's boss walking by. It is very rare to see him there, which is why I looked at the watch. I wondered where he could be going in our area.

In about six or seven minutes, my boss came to my office. He looked like someone who had been thoroughly chewed out. He told me, "You know I have always supported your move to Paris."

Of course, Joe's boss most adamantly opposed and did everything humanly possible to block Joe's move – and he was succeeding well at that subterfuge. What brought about the change?

The improbability of the turnabout, from hostility to support

Direct appeal by Joe to his boss was useless. That only seemed to make the boss even more determined that Joe not get his chance to go to Paris on the important assignment.

Mediation by the personnel office was not getting anywhere. The career officer was outranked by Joe's boss: "Who are you to tell me what is good for the organization?"

Paris office could put in its two cents worth as the receiving office. However, Joe was adamant that they not be told about the obstructionist strategy of his boss.

All roads seemed to be closed. Unless Joe could get his annual leave immediately to dedicate to winding up his affairs in Washington, renting his house, arranging shipment of household goods, he could simply not get to Paris in the ten-day period.

Here starts a chain of utterly improbable events.

Joe's boss's boss travels in Europe. He visits the Paris office. The one person in Paris who knows how important Joe is to the Paris office, and knows the critical time factor in his getting there on schedule, gets a sufficiently high-ranking person to impress upon Joe's boss's boss the imperative need to have Joe released. The boss's boss returns to Washington over the weekend. He decides to handle the Joe matter as the very first thing he would do. He walks over to Joe's boss's office. The step was so unusual that Joe checks his watch at that moment. On direct orders from the boss's boss, Joe's boss ceases from his obstructionism. The logjam is broken. Joe can move.

Thank God for "small" miracles!

The Precognition

While we mortals do not know what will happen in the very next moment, if God so chooses, He can let us a have a peek into the future. An hour and a half before its most unlikely occurrence, the miracle of the facilitating of Joe's transfer situation was indicated. The hopelessness of the situation adds to the dramatic impact of the assurance that there would be a positive development at 9:45 A.M. on Monday.

The Lord of the Universe is certainly the Lord of Time. Praise Him for the lifting of the veil of the future on special occasions for the assurance of His continuing care for us in our daily needs.

#19. Answered professional need: Guilty verdict reversed in retrial; lost job replaced – 1986 (exact time)

One Thursday, I received a call from the shepherd of the soprano section. A shepherd is someone who contacts members on short-notice events, and someone whom the members can contact with prayer requests for pressing personal needs.

That was the first time ever in two years that the soprano shepherd contacted me, a tenor. She referred to "Jane's" court case that was scheduled for the following Wednesday. Jane had called the shepherd to pray with her before the 7:30 P.M. rehearsal on Thursday. The shepherd asked if Jane would like anybody else to pray with her, and she had asked for me.

The distressing case

Eight months previously, at 1:20 A.M., Jane heard what sounded like a gang fight going on in the parking lot of her apartment building, right below her bedroom. The shouted exchanges made it clear that drugs were at the heart of the fight. The police came later, forty minutes after Jane called them four times. Before they came, they drove past the parking lot for eight minutes, which let the gangs disperse without being caught with the goods. Jane was quite frightened at the gang war noises, and she was furious at the long delay of the police to respond to her repeated calls. She went down to the parking lot and exclaimed to the officers: "What took you so long? I called you so many times! The gangs all got away because it took you so long!"

The woman police officer beamed her flashlight right into Jane's eyes and said: "Have you got any identification?" "I am the one who called you," said Jane as she tried to move away the flashlight which was shining right into her eyes. The woman officer and two male officers pinned Jane's arms to her back, pushed her to the ground, and snapped handcuffs on her. Jane's 15-year-old son saw his mother being pinned down, and he jumped to defend her. One of his friends. who was staying overnight, strong-armed him and prevented the son from assaulting the officer. Over her severe protests, Jane was hustled off to jail and kept there overnight.

The next morning she was taken before the County Police Commissioner, who charged her with four crimes: assault and battery of a police officer, resisting arrest, disorderly conduct, and failure to identify oneself to a uniformed officer. He released her on her own recognizance.

The trial

Three months later, Jane was brought before the District Court. The judge said that Jane was guilty on all four counts. But he did not seem to believe that she assaulted the woman police officer, in spite of corroboration by the male police officer. The judge offered probation and expunging of the record in three years if Jane would not press charges of false arrest. He finally sentenced her to five days in prison, and suspended the sentence.

Loss of job

The agony and humiliation of being arrested and kept in prison is bad enough. What is worse, now Jane has a criminal record. Despite Jane's explanation of what actually happened, her employer fired her. At the choir rehearsal on a Thursday, Jane got up and said" "I was fired from my job today. Please pray for me."

Inability to sleep, breathe

Jane was once attacked when she was 18. When the police closed in on her, she began reliving the trauma of that attack. The rough arrest and in the parking lot aggravated the sense of attack. Months afterwards,

Jane could not sleep due to nightmares. She had difficulty breathing. She underwent EKG examination for chest pains. Psychiatric sessions were not very helpful. Besides, she could not afford them.

Single parent

The crushing weight of this arrest and conviction had to be borne by herself, with no husband to share the burden. Further, she had to support her 15-year-old son.

Hiring a lawyer...

Jane decided to press for a new trial. The lawyer she hired appeared not to be motivated. He had not followed through the leads she had given him. In the meantime, witnesses who were solid to begin with seemed to waver as the trial date neared. One of the witnesses had moved away. All of them seemed to have forgotten numerous important details. And the lawyer who is supposed to orchestrate the entire case in Jane's behalf seemed not to care.

And firing him

With only three weeks to go before the trial, Jane fired her lawyer. In his place, she hired the lawyer's boss, who was assisted by her first lawyer. They pointed out that assault and battery of a police officer is a common law misdemeanor with a 99-year sentence! However, the jury could not impose a heavier sentence than that already imposed by the District Court Judge.

A new, better job

Mercifully, Jane was offered a new job over the telephone the very day she was fired from her previous job. With the new job, there were new pressures to perform well. And that at a time when the trial date was approaching. Hiring a new lawyer at the last moment increased her anxiety level.

De novo trial

The lawyers advised her that the trial would be *de novo*. The Latin phrase means, "Fresh from the start." Instead of the first trial by the judge, this would be a trial by the jury of one's peers. The transcript of the previous trial stands; the plaintiffs (police) could not modify their testimony. If they did, it could result in impeachment of their testimony.

The jury could not be informed that there was a previous trial, or that there was a guilty verdict at the trial by judge. If the jury were informed of either, it would mean an automatic mistrial.

Possible adverse outcome

Jane was scared that if her previously-solid witnesses began to weaken, and if some of the key witnesses could not be found, she could well lose her case. At the District Court trial, the arresting male police officer had backed up the female police officer's story of Jane assaulting her in pushing the flashlight away. Unless he told the truth, and knocked down the female police officer's fabrication, Jane's words alone would not suffice. The woman police officer had claimed that she did not know that Jane was the person who had called them, a story repeated by the male police officer. Unless the witnesses could establish that the police indeed knew that Jane was the one who had called them, the case could be lost. And with it, the criminal conviction would stand; and, the police could bring countersuit for expenses and damages.

His answer through his Word

It was in this context of serious concern that Jane asked the shepherd of the soprano section and me to pray with her six days before the trial. We met at 7:15 P.M. and had a short prayer session. I told them that I was entering a new experience in intercessory prayer. The identified answers described in *Interceding* claimed the promise of a verse in making the request. Now I have been finding that instead of claiming a promise, I have been receiving verses as identified answers.

Three Scripture verses as answer to intercession

As I prayed, two Scriptural references began to emerge. In addition, a third non-Scriptural message began to strongly suggest itself during the short prayer session immediately preceding the choir rehearsal. During the first half of the rehearsal, the messages came back, unbidden, in identical form. So, I wrote them out for Jane during the rehearsal break.

One reference was, "Truth shall make you free." (John 8: 32, KJV) Another was to the "pillar of fire and the pillar of cloud." Jane said she would locate the precise references at home using the concordance. The reference was:

> During the last watch of the night the LORD looked down from the pillar of fire and cloud at the Egyptian army and threw it into confusion. He made the wheels of their chariots come off so that they had difficulty driving. And the Egyptians said, "Let's get away from the Israelites! The LORD is fighting for them against Egypt." (Exodus 14:24-25, NIV)

Two days later, late Saturday night, I felt that I should look up the Scriptural references. Instead of the early recollection I had of the pillars of fire and cloud, I was gripped with a new verse which seemed custom-made for Jane. I was awakened after a short sleep. I explained to my wife that I had to put in writing the message for Jane.

"Victory verse"

Jane wrote a note to me saying: "First of all, thank you so much for praying with and for me, and also for the 'victory verse,' as I think of it, about the wheels of Pharaoh's chariots falling off!"

"Wheels of (Egyptian) chariots com(ing) off"

As I transmitted the message to Jane over the phone on Sunday, we felt that the central element was the confusion in the ranks of pursuing Egyptians, and loss of control over their own chariots because the wheels were falling off.

The judge's dismissal of two charges

The case came to trial around mid-afternoon and lasted until 5:50 P.M. the next day. The judge threw out one charge – failure to identify oneself to a uniformed officer – at the conclusion of the prosecutor's presentation of the case, even before Jane's defense began. Off came one wheel!

At the conclusion of the presentation of the plaintiff's case, the judge threw out another charge – disorderly conduct to the disturbance of public peace – as being too ridiculous. Off came another wheel!

Confusion in the ranks of the police

The woman police officer had charged that Jane assaulted a police officer, and resisted arrest when she pushed the flashlight she beamed into Jane's eyes. The woman police officer flashed the light asking Jane, "Do you have some identification?" Now that the charge of Jane's refusal to identify herself to a police officer was already dismissed by the Judge, the assault charge became moot. Off came the third wheel!

The woman police officer had additionally claimed that Jane had attacked the male police officer and tore off his shirt, which was backed up by him at the District Court trial. Contradicting his own testimony at the first trial, the male police officer now said that somebody tore off his shirt, but he could not say that it was Jane. The attacker tore it off from behind, so he could not see the person. No torn shirt was produced; there was no witness. Off came the fourth wheel!

Jury verdict: "Not guilty"

The jury found Jane "Not guilty" on both the counts. Her record was expunged. The truth indeed set her free. The 3478-year-old promise of the victory verse was entirely fulfilled! Praise the Lord!

KEY WORDS: Miracle; Gideon's Rule; Recompensing Resources

Discussion Starters – Chapter 6

1. How do you apply Gideon's rule in practice?

2. Sketch the miraculous in unblocking "Joe's" promotion and transfer.

3. Apply the victory verse to "Jane's" Case.

4. Explain precognition. Relate it to Ch. 3 discussion of exact time.

5. How would you characterize the timeframe of "Jane's" new job?

6. Review 3 KEY WORDS: Miracle; Gideon's rule; recompensing resource

Share a divine message you transmitted pertaining to exact/expectant time.

7

Recompensing Resources For Exact Time II

Thankfully recognizing that it is the Infinite God alone Who elevates to utmost significance our relatively insignificant needs, we recount different types of concrete needs which require different types of resources.

Exact time

The Lord's answers in exact time is recalled with respect to two professional needs in Chapter 6, and with respect to one each of financial, physical, relational, and spiritual needs in Chapter 7.

#20. Answered relational need: Prayer support provided from Bombay, India half a world away at precise moment of unspecified need in Bethesda, Maryland: 1987 (exact time)

In July 1987, I was travelling overseas to make presentations on artificial intelligence and technology transfer. En route, I flew from Rangoon to Calcutta. After the speeches, interviews, and reception I got to bed near midnight, only to be awakened at 3 A.M. to get ready to go to the airport to fly to Bombay, 1500 miles west. No sooner did I arrive than the new round of activities began. Based on careful records of sleep including shut-eye on the plane, I was averaging 3½ hours of sleep in 24 hours.

The next morning I woke up. I looked at my watch and found the time was 7:30 A.M. I did not have to get up at that time for the first morning appointment. And I certainly could use more sleep. Then why wake up?

I had a strong, unmistakable sense that "Jeannie" needed my prayers half a world away in Bethesda, Maryland. Prayers for what? I was not given any specific concrete need to pray for; simply that she needed prayer support. When it is Sunday July 12, 7:30 A.M. in Bombay, what time is it in Bethesda? I mused: 7:30 P.M. on July 11? What is happening on a Saturday night that needed urgent prayer support?

The next month when I got back from my speaking tour, I asked Jeannie: "What was happening at 7:30 P.M. on Saturday, July 11? I woke up in Bombay with a strong sense that you needed immediate prayer support. I figured that it was 7:30 P.M. on Saturday your time."

Jeannie beamed. "That was when 'Ted' was picking me up. I was so nervous. I did not know how it would go. Thank you for praying for me. It went fine."

This particular date was the first in two years. After several months, "Ted" proposed to Jeannie and a date was set for the wedding.

#21. Answered physical need: Prayer support from Taipei, Taiwan at precise moment of unspecified need at camp 30 miles away: 1984 (exact time)

In Taipei, Tuesday prayer breakfasts have been held by Yoke Fellows under the Rev. John Brantingham for many years. One morning, John said, "If during this week, you feel that you have to pray for someone, do it; it is the Lord prodding you." That Saturday noon – 12:05 P.M.- I suddenly felt gripped by a need to pray urgently for "Timmy." I had no idea what his need was, but I felt I should pray then and there for Timmy's need whatever it might be. After a few minutes, I felt compelled to pray for him again, and I did.

Two days later, I saw him just before the start of the church council meeting on Monday evening. I asked him: "What was the urgent problem that you had on Saturday at 12:05?" He said, "I went to camp on Friday evening with some Chinese young people. From time to time I get these severe headaches when the pain at the base of my neck can be excruciating. On Saturday just after 12, I remember dashing to the bathroom with excruciating pain and vomiting. But right after that I was fine."

#22. Answered spiritual need: Prayer support from Bethesda, Maryland at precise moment of unspecified need in Taipei, Taiwan: 1985 (exact time)

Eloise Harder has been a missionary in Taiwan with The Evangelical Alliance Mission (TEAM) since the '70s. The Bethany School which she has served in various capacities teaches some 175-200 children of Chinese and Asian families working in Taiwan. A majority of children come from non-Christian families, but the families choose to let their children be taught at a Christian School. The seeds sown so early in their lives often bear fruit as shared in Eloise's letter of August 1992:

> I would like to share part of a letter I received this summer from an Indian family – the first in the school-who have become very special to me. Their 3 children all graduated this year, son #1 from college in Australia, son #2 from high school (I was there!) and their daughter from our 8th grade.

> "We are glad that all three of our children spent the better part of their schooling years at Bethany. Here is hoping that the positive influence of the values they learnt will guide them through the rest of their lives. A big thank you to all the teachers and staff at Bethany! Most of all, we thank YOU, Miss Harder, for truly being our friend, guide and philosopher for the past 15 years or more..." The daughter is a Christian and son #2 I think is also, but I don't think #1 is. The parents are Hindu. What a privilege, and responsibility, to work with these young people and their parents.

I returned home from my second term of Fulbright professorship in Taiwan in August, 1985. Three months later, during the Wednesday before Thanksgiving, I suddenly felt I had to pray urgently for Elosie in Taiwan for something in connection with her mission. I prayed for her support in the unspecified need. I felt two more times during the day to urgently uphold her in prayer, and I did.

The following April, I was in Taipei briefly. When I saw Eloise after church, I asked her if she had any problem around Thanksgiving the year before. No, she couldn't think of anything. Then she suddenly remembered. "Yes, it was during Thanksgiving Week. We have a caretaker at Bethany who regards me as a daughter. He has been with us for many years. Suddenly he told me that he was quitting last November. That was very upsetting, because if we couldn't find a good caretaker, the school itself would have to be shut down. (That makes the problem primarily spiritual, because Eloise's mission itself was threatened if the school were to be shut down) And we couldn't afford to pay any more to someone else even if we could find someone. It was a big problem for us for several days. Thank God, it was resolved when he decided to stay."

KEY WORDS: Exact Time, Veil of Time, Recompnesing Resources

Discussion Starters – Chapter 7

1. Review "God lifting the veil of time" in chapter 5.

2. Is a divine message meeting a specific need in exact time harder than one meeting a need in expectant time? Why?

3. How does the compelling urge to pray for someone far away in time and space different from telepathy or extra-sensory perception?

4. Consider again the question: When we ask the Lord to meet a concrete need in exact time, are we giving the Lord an "ultimatum?"

5. Review 3 KEY WORDS: exact time, veil of time, recompensing resources

8

Renewing Resources For Expectant Time I

Thankfully recognizing that it is the Infinite God alone Who elevates to utmost significance our relatively insignificant needs, we recount different types of concrete needs that require different types of resources.

Expectant time

The Lord's answers in expectant time are recalled with respect to one physical need, one professional need, and two relational needs in Chapter 8, and with respect to one physical, and one spiritual need in Chapter 9.

Taipei International Church – Becoming a praying church

On the first Sunday in September, 1983, Pastor Mike VanderPol of Taipei International Church (TIC) said in his sermon, "I want TIC to become a praying church." Nudging my wife sitting next to me, I said, "That is my mission." Writes Pastor VanderPol:

> In a recent worship service, I challenged the congregation of Taipei International Church to become a praying church. At the end of the service, Dr. Chacko came over and said that he had a plan to follow up on that challenge. Within a matter of weeks he filled the Sunday school room to overflowing as he explained in his scientific way the whole matter of praying. Out of this experience came not only the making of intercessory prayer, a now-integral part of our morning worship, but also this book (*Interceding with the Infinite: Practicing Prayer Power*), which is an expanded exposition of the eight-week course on prayer....
> Here is an intriguing book on intercessory prayer...[I]t challenges the mind, it is filled with stimulating

> thoughts on practical aspects of prayer. George speaks of dimensions of prayer which directly link finite man with the Infinite God...
>
> I recommend this book because we've seen its principles come to life in Taipei International Church...The last chapter outlines how you, your cell group or your church can richly benefit from this book in seeing the power of God at work within our lives through praying for one another.

Make prayer power work for you!
As we started the eight-week course on intercessory prayer, we committed ourselves to start public prayer for private needs beginning in March, 1984.

#23. Answered physical need: One-and-a-half-year old Lynette's right tear duct blocked from birth – 1984 (expectant time)

In the seventh week of our intercession, there was an anonymous request for prayer for 1½-year-old child with a blocked tear duct from birth.

From claiming a promise—TIC...

As I prayed for a promise to claim, I was given Matthew 19:14. I examine different translations to see which one (or more) translation speaks most directly to the situation. I settled on Moffatt and King James Version jointly: "Let the children alone, do not stop them from coming to me: for of such is the kingdom of heaven." (Matthew 19:14, MOF, KJV)

Promise and Petition
Claiming the promise, we present the petition:

> Oh Christ, who said, "Let the children alone, do not stop them from coming to me, for of such is the kingdom of heaven," we bring to Thee 1½-year-old Lynnette with the blocked tear duct in her right eye, and pray for Thy healing upon the little one.

Return to the States; Back to Taipei in the Fall
I left Taipei in April, but returned in October on a second Fulbright. At the pastor's suggestion, I called on the Deputy General Manager of Singapore National Bank to invite him to join the TIC Council. He thanked me for praying for Lynnette. "She is my daughter," he said. They

had gone to all the specialists they could find in Singapore and elsewhere for a year and a half, with no result. His wife had put in the request for intercession for Lynnette on the first Sunday they were in Taipei on his new assignment. I had no idea that she was his daughter.

A Neighbor's Casual Invitation

He said that the very next day after the public intercession, a neighbor was going to the doctor. She asked Lynnette's mother if she wanted to go along. She did. It turned out that the doctor had been working on a simple procedure. He said that the tear duct could be unblocked with a relatively simple operation, and her right eye was restored!

TIC forming the God triangle with Lynnette

Later when I was asked to write an article on Prayer for the TIC *Chimes,* I raised the question: Why couldn't anyone during the 18 months restore the child's right eye? Certainly, the best specialists in Singapore and elsewhere were contacted. Did it mean that TIC was special? No, it only meant that God gave us the privilege to become a community of intercession to mediate His miracle. To Him be the praise and glory!

...to receiving promissory words as identified answers—Fourth

At Fourth Presbyterian Church, we had a different experience. Instead of promises being the means, they became the end. The promises themselves became the identified answers, instead of being the claims to the answers.

The promise is a particular verse(s). Imagine a verse relating to an event that took place in B.C. 1491 in the Middle East, in an agrarian economy. How can that apply in 1986, in the United States of America, the seat of high-technology research? In Chapter 5, we already saw how every word of a verse dated B.C. 1491 came true almost 3,500 years later!

#24. Answered professional need: Professional unemployed for 913 days – 1984 (expectant time)

At the end of the third Sunday of the class on intercessory prayer, "Joe's" closest friend "Joan" came up and said that Joe and his wife were Joan's best friends. They had been urging her to come to the class. She had attended the class the previous week for the first time, which she found to be everything her friends said it would be. She wanted to say hello the previous week, but there were so many waiting to talk that she felt uneasy adding to their number. But this Sunday, she told herself, she was going to come up and talk.

The Need

She said almost in passing: "I have no job. I have had to sell all my jewelry. I had been sick for months, and by the time I got out of the hospital, my job was gone. Please pray for me." There was no discernible urgency in her voice. It almost sounded as though she was talking about someone else. But she seemed genuine in her request. I felt led to pray for her.

The Promise

I prayed for Joan whom I remembered by face rather than by name. The next day, I had a message for her. I should tell her to read 1 Kings 17:13.

The Transmittal

In transmitting God's specific messages for specific persons, I must be absolutely scrupulous in adding nothing and subtracting nothing. It is the Lord who is speaking to that person; therefore, the message must mean something specific to that person. It may sound like gibberish to others, but to the intended one, that message would be sweet music.

But to deliver the message, I must first find out her name, which I recalled only vaguely, having met her among others after the class. But recalling that she was a friend of Joe's, I tried reaching him, but without success. Other efforts to find out who she was and how I could reach her on Monday and Tuesday did not succeed.

Tuesday evening I felt I had to get the message to her urgently. This time I was able to reach Joe who was glad to give me Joan's number. I felt I had to reach her by 9:40 P.M. And I dialed her number.

The phone was picked up on the second ring. I identified myself, and said that I had a message for her. Would she get her Bible? I told her the verse, which she read aloud. She was not familiar with the story of Elijah and the widow of Zarephath. I felt I knew part of the meaning of that verse, but it was not my place to interpret it for her; she had to get the interpretation herself.

Background: Divorced; unemployed for 2½ years

At the end of our brief conversation after the class, Joan had introduced her 12-year-old son to me. I thought that he had attended Sunday school while his mother attended adult Sunday school, probably to be picked up by his father who could be attending another adult Sunday school class.

When I reached her by phone on Tuesday evening, Joan said she had just come home from attending the class at Fourth for divorced and separated parents. She said she was sitting on her bed with her head on her knees, saying : "Lord, I am at the end of my rope. I don't know what to do. Lord…" And the telephone rang.

Things have been terrible and there seemed to be no hope. She had sent out two hundred copies of her resumé, and there were two or three answers. And once she got to the interview, the refrain was the same: "You are too qualified. Our job is way below what you have been doing. Sorry." When she offers to start low, they would say: "No, we can't do that; you are overqualified for that position."

At that moment, she was working at an executive search company, at her own expense. She would have to call up currently employed senior people, talk them into leaving for some other position elsewhere for a higher salary, and her firm would get the commission only after spiriting someone away. She felt that the lies that had to be told even to get to talk to the senior executives were demeaning, making her quite unhappy to carry on at that place. Every call she made was being monitored by the boss to make sure that she was sufficiently persuasive.

She had indeed risen to great heights in the government, holding the position of special assistant to the Assistant Secretary of one of the U.S. Cabinet departments. The normal tenure is two years, but she had been able to hold it for twice as long. However, the change of administration pushed her out by new claimants to the position. The trauma of hanging on to the job, and the incessant intrigues had been internalized to such a degree that they erupted in the form of a serious spinal affliction which required prolonged hospitalization. By the time she got out of the hospital, her replacement was long in place.

That was 2½ years ago.

The divorce occurred before her losing battle for her professional position which had been her pride and joy. She lost her house, and had to move into a very small place with her son, whom the father refused to see since he was 4. That left the boy scarred for life. Whenever his mother lost another possible job opening, the son would feel guilty and depressed, blaming him for the failure. He has had to be sent to a special school which cost $8,000 a year in tuition alone.

The grave story came out over the phone. She was hitting her head against her knee on the bed out of desperation, not knowing where to turn. "Just when I called out 'Lord' a second time, the phone rang, and you answered. It gave me goose pimples."

New resumé

The anxiety attacks of her son, the cramped living conditions, the scramble for daily necessities, and her own shattered ego all centered around the one problem: a satisfactory job. The first step toward finding a satisfactory job is an effective resumé.

Since two hundred copies of her current resumé had not brought any significant response, it was evident that a new resumé had to be developed. It should be a means not just to find a job, but rather to find a career. That should start with Joan's view of what her talents are, and what she, as their steward, should do with them.

Two and a half years of recurring disappointments made Joan seriously question her talents. But time was of the essence. She said she would meet with me the very next morning, Wednesday.

Writing resumés is not my profession. However, I have worked with close friends and family to develop resumés with a difference. Instead of making them a litany of what they had done in the past, the focus is on the future: what would they like best to do? To the Christian, I put the question: "What are your talents?" Together, we seek to discover the special aptitudes and abilities, the application of which gives them the best sense of fulfillment. How best can they be expressed in terms of a recognizable job description? I put myself in the position of an attorney, trying to put the best "case" for my "client".

The resumé has to fit the "client". Otherwise, he cannot use it. King Saul, desperate to find someone to fight Goliath in single combat and save Israel, was overjoyed at finding the shepherd boy, David. The king gave him his own armor, the highest token of honor and trust. But David could not use the sophisticated armament, because that was not David's style:

> Saul dressed David in his own tunic. He put a coat of armor on him and a bronze helmet on his head. David buckled his sword over his coat and tried to walk, but in vain, for he was not used to such armor. So David said to Saul, "I cannot move with these; I am not used to them. " And David put them off; he grasped his club, picked five smooth stones form the stream and put them in the shepherd's bag that served him for a knapsack, took his sling in his hand, and went to meet the Philistine." (1 Samuel 17: 38-40, MOF, NIV)

It took an entire day to discover what Joan's talents were, and how much of what she had done was applicable to her career objective. She felt reassured that the long 2½ years in the professional wilderness did not make her "right hand forget its skill." (Psalm 137:5, NIV)

"First make a small cake of bread for me" (1 Kings 17:13, NIV)

Joan's situation was desperate. She did not know how she would pay rent, how she would buy groceries, how she would pay her son's tuition, how she could keep up her car payments, or how she could pay for her medicine. The verse that I transmitted to her must have sounded somewhat strange. Here was the widow of Zarephath who could make two cakes of bread, one each for for herself and her son for their last meal before they died. And here is Elijah, asking that half of all her earthly wherewithal to be first given to him!

> And Elijah said unto her, "Fear not. Go home and do as you have said. But first make a small cake of bread for me from what you have and bring it to me here, and then make something for yourself and your son. For this is what the LORD, the God of Israel, says: 'The jar of flour will not be used up and the jug of oil will not run dry until the day the LORD gives rain on the land." (1 Kings 17:13-14, KJV, MOF, NIV)

Give first, then receive

I did not know what Joan could actually give in her extreme situation of want. However, I felt when I was given the message, that she would have first to be the giver before she would receive. I was confident that the renewing resource clearly meant a professional job which would pay her a decent salary on a regular basis, although I did not mention either of the interpretations to her.

She first talked to me on September 28. I gave her the message two days later. On October 2nd, I carried two copies of her resumé in person to two members of my Kiwanis Club, asking if they could give her any leads in their organizations or others. I followed up the contacts and tried two additional contacts in the club as well. Joan was passing the new resumé around also. But no promising developments.

It looked as though Elijah had to get his small cake first.

#25. Answered relational need: Initiation of broken communications – 1984 (expectant time)

Another member of the intercessory prayer class, "Jim" called me on Columbus Day, October 13, to tell me that as he was doing his Bible study and devotions, he felt directed to call me and tell me of a serious situation.

For several years, Jim had been talking to "Jason" about Jesus Christ. Jason is an exceptionally brilliant man, who has achieved a great deal of success and renown in his professional field. He married late in life, and had two beautiful little boys. He has been drifting apart from his wife for some time, and had decided to divorce her. Jim talked to both Jason and his wife and had been urging Jason to restore his relationship with her.

Two days earlier, when Jim went to see Jason, he told Jim, "I feel like taking the machine gun to the office and taking down several people with me." Coming from a highly intelligent man who had built up a highly successful career, and who took great pride in his rational capabilities, suicidal threats were shocking. Jim talked at some length about the power of Christ. Jason talked of going to his sister who had a

Ph. D. in psychology, and who lived out of state.

On Monday, October 13, when Jim called, Jason's little boy said that his dad had not returned home since Saturday. That was when Jim called me to ask for my prayers.

Two days later, Joan called late in the evening, quite down. She had to arrange for movers to take her furniture out of a friend's house immediately, since the friend had prospective tenants coming to look at the house. Joan had no money for the movers. In fact, her electricity was going to be cut off that morning, and she sent them a check which had to be covered. Even if she could find a mover, he would have to be paid cash; and further, she had to find a warehouse where she could store the furniture since there was no room in her small apartment

Joan did not know Jason. But it came to me that she could probably talk to him about his planned divorce, because she herself had gone through a divorce. I suggested that if Jason were intrigued, he could think of some new venture where Joan's talents could be put to productive use. The chances of Jason having a job for Joan were very slight, but the challenge to think about someone else's problem would help him to get out of his preoccupation with himself.

I asked Jim to pray about the possibility that Joan could see Jason. The next day, after talking it over with both parties, Joan called Jason to make an appointment. They met on Friday.

While Joan's need for a job was the agenda, Jason spent most of the time talking about his problems with his wife. Joan was later surprised to find how vigorous she was in talking to Jason: "You can't divorce your wife. Have you given her half the time and attention you give to your job? You cannot talk about divorce until you have tried your best. I bet you can get her do whatever you want her to do."

That was Elijah's small cake. Joan took time away from her work to meet with a total stranger, and talk to him with conviction about his problem, and bring some measure of helpful perspective to him.

"Then make something for yourself and your son"

Even as Joan was setting up the meeting with Jason, an interview opportunity was opening up. If successful, Joan would work for three days. I could not get excited about three days of work, but to someone who has had no work, even three days of consulting would be most welcome. The appointment was moved to the following week.

At the interview, the prospective employer told Joan what kind of capabilities she was looking for in the new high-level employee. Joan heard the exact words that Joan had in her new resumé. In other words, Joan was exactly whom the employer was looking for! Subsequent interviews had to be held to work out the terms. The 2,915 year-old promissory words were fulfilled to the letter! Joan was ecstatic. "Exactly what I wanted to do all my life. And it is even in the very same building that I had wanted to work in!" In 23 days, Joan found the job which she had not been able to get in 913 days! The promissory words were fulfilled to the letter. She first ministered to someone else, Jason, whom God sent her way. And she herself was first given recurring resources in the form of three days of consulting work, which grew to four days a week, converting the job from a one-time effort to a regular, if part-time, work. By the end of the year, the job became full-time, making it into a renewing resource.

KEY WORDS: Expectant Time, Veil of Time, Renewing Resources

Discussion Starters- Chapter 8

1. Why does God want us sometime to give before we receive?

2. How do we guard against our own sympathies with the given situation corrupting the divine message for the need?

3. What is the difference between a praying church and any church which offers prayers at various worship services?

4. We saw in Chapter 2 that when Jesus told the disciples, "Give ye them to eat," their resources were far too small to meet the need. Yet Jesus says: one, access your resources (How many loaves do you have?); two, offer them to the Lord. Discuss the offering of one's own resources in #25 and #26.

5. Review 3 KEY WORDS: Expectant Time, Veil of Time, Renewing Resources

Share a divine message you transmitted pertaining to exact/expectant time.

9

Renewing Resources for Expectant Time II

Thankfully recognizing that it is the Infinite God alone Who elevates to utmost significance our relatively insignificant needs, we recount different types of concrete needs which require different types of resources.

Expectant time

The Lord's answers in expectant time are recalled with respect to one physical need, one professional need, and two relational needs in Chapter 8, and with respect to one Physical, and one Spiritual need in Chapter 9.

#26. Answered physical need: Recovery from the point of death – 1991 (expectant time)

When I returned from a committee meeting, my wife said, "Sam called around 6:30 A.M. from California. The message is on the phone." I said, "That is 3:30 in the morning in California. It must be very urgent."

And it was. Sam's message was: "Nancy called me saying, 'My father is dying. Please pray for him.'"

Later Sam would tell our men's retreat in March 1992: "My wife called me in California. She said, 'My father is dying.' She was speaking not as a daughter, but as a medical doctor. She refused the hospital permission to put her father on life-sustaining devices. She was distraught and was telling me the situation at 3:15 in the morning, California time. I made two calls. I called George Chacko, and I called Jeff Jeremiah (Executive Pastor of Fourth), and asked them to pray for my father-in-law.

Nancy Jones, M.D. is the chief anesthesiologist with Kaiser Permanente Medical Center, Kensington, Maryland. Her father had been receiving the best medical care possible, the specialists from all the departments at the Center sparing no effort to help the father of a colleague. But he was sinking.

What should I pray for? Should I pray to spare Mr. McCrary's life? I prayed that if it be the Lord's will, Mr. McCrary be healed, and that he may be comfortable in his illness.

In April, I asked what her father's chances of recovery at that time was. She said it was less than 1%. In other words, the odds were 100 to 1 against his not living at that time. He was in fact flatlined, which meant that his body had stopped functioning. But the Lord spared McCrary. His rapid deterioration suddenly stopped. Nancy could not explain what happened. Her father opened his eyes and began to recover. In a few days he went home. Sam told me that after his recovery, his father-in-law was able to mend some relationships. When I returned in July from an extended overseas trip, I saw Nancy. She said her father had died a few weeks earlier. "He was at peace," she said.

#27 Answered physical need: Large cyst disappearing just prior to scheduled hysterectomy – 1996 (expectant time)

On Sunday, September 15, Janelle, convenor of the prayer chain at St. Andrew's Presbyterian Church, Kuala Lumpur, handed me a prayer request card and said, "Here's something you can sink your teeth into – a tough situation." The handwritten request said, "I am 6-weeks pregnant with my second baby. The doctor discovered a cyst in my womb. No medicine will help. But God can make it disappear. Please pray for me." Signed Elizabeth Lee. The Sep 9 sonogram shows a grapefruit-sized cyst hiding the baby completely.

Intercession

I had never met her. When Janelle gave me the card, I sensed I should pray for Elizabeth. I prayed for her healing if it be His will.

The Message

Tuesday morning, when I was getting ready to go to the office, the phrase "touch the hem of his garment" came to mind. It referred to the woman who had been subject to bleeding for 12 years, in Matthew 9:20-22.

The Meaning

I delivered the message to her, and asked her, What does that tell you? The message is between the Lord and you." She said, "I have to do something. She reached out and touched Him." Elizabeth Lee said she had to reach out and do something.

Making the "Small cake"

It was six weeks later before I had called Elizabeth Lee and asked if she had followed up on her understanding of the message, that she should do something. She said, "Oh, I had forgotten that! I thought I just needed to have faith."

I suggested that while God does not need our offerings to work his miracles, nevertheless, He asks us to search our own resources. Elijah asked the widow of Zarephath to bake him a small cake before she ate her last meal. She found her supply of flour and oil were daily replenished during the entire famine.

Later, Elizabeth Lee told me that it was right after my discussion of the small cake that she changed her mind about attending a healing service. "I was not keen to go there because too many of my students would be there, and I didn't want to share such intimate problems with them. After I spoke to you, I had a different sense of the small cake. You told me that for a Jewish woman to touch a man, and a Rabbi at that, was quite out of character. But she did it. So also, I should do something out of character for me. I went to the church too charismatic for my taste. The pastor simply prayed for each person who needed healing. I (George) asked, "Did you feel anything?" She said no.

After the service, the pastor said, "Does anyone know if Sunway College has a hall?" – for their revival service. Elizabeth said that it had. "Because I was there that night, I could make sure that the hall, which was under construction, would be ready when the church wanted it. No one else could. That was the small cake."

The healing

Elizabeth Lee called me early in the morning on November 8. "Last night, I went to my doctor, who had scheduled me for a hysterectomy on November 15. He said, 'Elizabeth, the cyst has shrunk so small that I cannot even find it.' Praise the Lord!"

#28 Answered relational need: Financial catastrophe of engaged couple reversed before wedding – 1996 (expectant time)

When I e-mailed the preceding testimony to the Rev. Dr. Nathan Showalter, who is pastor of Taipei International Church, he made a prayer request in November, 1996 by e-mail:

> George, I am giving pre-marital counseling to a couple, she's Indian Chinese, he's Taiwanese. She's Christian. He's Taoist. They plan to be married on Dec. 25. They've suffered a serious business reversal in their fledgling trading company. Sent a container full of Christmas lights to Greece in good faith, only to discover that the agent had not done his homework on standards, and now the lights cannot clear customs. This will almost put them out of business, and not

in very good shape financially for the wedding.
Pray that the crisis might join them in faith, and draw them closer to each other and to God.
Names are Peter & Marilyn.
Thanks!
Nate

From chacko Tue Nov 12 07:59:55 1996
To: NShowalter
Subject: Re: Prayer Request
"Go higher up" is the repeated message I get for Peter and Marilyn. Tell his agent to "Go higher up." They should ask the Lord what it means.

From chacko Tue Nov 28 17:27:03 1996
To: NShowalter
Subject: Re: Prayer Request
Nate, Since yesterday, I have had to intercede for Peter and Marilyn several times. I sense that Peter feels that if he stays with the familiar Taoism he would not be experiencing the difficulties they are having (in business). Perhaps Marilyn has already asked for your help. If not, you might consider giving her a call.
George

From: NShowalter Thu Nov 28 19:43 GMT 1996
To: chacko
Subject: Re: Prayer Request
I called Peter and Marilyn the day before yesterday. They were excited over the miracle that God has done. The shipment cleared customs without their doing anything. They have received payment. They are so excited and seem to be giving full credit to God.
I told them about your prayers and your word from God.
Thank you, George!
They plan to be married on Dec. 22 or 24.
Please pray that Peter will make a clear commitment to Christ before then.
Thanks,
Nate

#29 Answered professional need: Regional manager abruptly out of a job gets confirmation of Scriptural message – 1996 (expectant time)

Just before I left Malaysia for the States in December, 1996, a member of my intercessory prayer workshop unexpectedly lost his job. The blow was particularly hard because he had come from Manila two years earlier, and was appointed as the regional manager for all of southeast Asia. In two years, he had built up the business. The boss from the States had arrived on a year-end inspection. Unbeknownst to "Jacob," the boss had brought with him someone to take over the job. Jacob, a man of reserve, shared with me his predicament. I prayed for him, and got a message, which I e-mailed to him on December 10:

> As you know, I wait for a specific message to be repeated, unbidden - i.e., when I am NOT thinking about the intercessory situation - two times or more in identical form. You also know that I diligently search the particular translation from which the message came. Here is the message for you:
> They made their way through Phyrgia and the Galatia district, since the Holy Spirit prevented them from speaking God's message in the province of Asia. When they approached Mysia they tried to enter Bithynica, but the Spirit of Jesus would not allow them. Acts 16:6-7 (Phillips)
> "Tried to enter…not allow" was the first phrase that came to me. And then the fact that it was the second place they were directed away from.
> Ask the Lord what He means.
> Yours In Him,
> George.

Jacob e-mailed in January 16:

> Though I still don't know which door God is shutting closed at me, I rest in the knowledge that He is looking after me and will shut those doors that He doesn't want me to go through, as he shut the Clorox door. This is why I believe so. On January 9, I wrote a letter to our family and friends to tell them about what was happening to our lives (a copy of which was e-mailed to you separately). On January 10 (exactly a month after your message to me on Dec 10, see copy below) a friend replied via fax with a copy of a reading for the day taken from some daily Bible reading book. And guess what? The verse reading for that day was Acts 16:6, the exact same verse in your message to me. And the reading goes on to explain what the verse means. I've tried to attach his fax to this message but just in case I have not done it right, here is what the reading says about that verse:

"Beloved, whenever you are doubtful as to your course, submit your judgment absolutely to the Spirit of God, and ask Him to shut against you every door but the right one. Say,
'Blessed Spirit, I cast on thee the entire responsibility of closing against me any and every course which is not of God. Let me hear Thy voice behind me whenever I turn to my right hand or the left.'
"In the meantime, continue along the path which you have been already treading. Abide in the calling in which you are called, unless you are clearly told to do something else. The Spirit of Jesus waits to be to you, O pilgrim, what He was to Paul. Only be careful to obey His least prohibitions; and where after believing prayer, there are no apparent hindrances, go forward with enlarged heart. Do not be surprised if the answer comes in closed doors. But when the doors are shut right and left, an open road is sure to lead to Troas. There Luke awaits, and visions will point the way, where vast opportunities stand open, and faithful friends are waiting."
From "Paul," by Meyer.
George, if this is not God speaking, clarifying for me the message you originally conveyed to me then I don't know when He does. It is so affirming to actually hear the voice of God in the way He chooses to speak to us. Now I know what God wants me to do: prayerfully move forward on my present course and be sensitive to hindrances or openness that He puts in our way.

#30 Answered professional need: Utterly frustrated professional looking for the Lord's guidance – 1997 (expectant time)

Another stalwart member of my intercessory workshop e-mailed me on career guidance in January, 1997:

George,
It was really a blessing that you arrived in St. Andrews when you did as I have personally benefitted enormously from your teaching and guidance. I have prayed that the spirit of confusion that has plagued me for the past few years will be cast out and that my career direction will become clearer to me in time. My most pressing

prayer need is in the area of my career. I am unable to generate any enthusiasm for my job and I cannot see any positions in the company that I can happily fill (one of the reasons for the stall in my career is my refusal to accept several positions offered to me because it involved working for a manager that I feel is unprincipled and vindictive).

As a consequence of this, I have not been able to perform as efficiently as I am capable of doing in my present position. I have often considered a change of career but my several efforts to do this have not been successful and I am beginning to think that the Lord does not plan for me to leave the company I presently work for. I have been praying for the Lord to show me his plan for me especially as far as my career is concerned and the present situation has been detrimental to my professional endeavors as I am confused and unfocused. The positive side is that the Managing Director of the company has recognized that I have some problems and has been very patient with me.
I often feel that my problem is trivial and that I am merely going through a readjustment of my career priorities. I have no wish to travel extensively nor do I want to work outside Malaysia. Unfortunately, to the present company I am with, these are important employee attributes. At present, I have applied to a local company that is slated to be given the contract to develop the Malaysian smart card, to work in the smart card technology division If this position comes through, it will be welcome.
I look forward to seeing you again soon in Malaysia.
God bless....

I replied:

I saw your e-mail of Jan 26, 2:49 a.m. at 7:20 a.m. local time on January 26. When we discussed your career in your car when you kindly drove me back to UPM in April, I prayed about it, but received no message. Today, almost as soon as I finished praying for you, I got a message. As you know, I wait for a specific message to be repeated, unbidden - i.e., when I am NOT thinking about the intercessory

```
situation - two or more times in identical
form. You also know that I diligently
search for the particular translations
from which the message comes. Here is the
message for you:

"And he said unto them, 'Cast the net on
the right side of the ship, and you'll
have a catch.'" (John 21:6, King James
Version, J.B. Phillips).
The phrase that came to mind was "Cast the
net on the right side of the ship."
Ask the Lord what He means.
```

KEY WORDS: Renewing resources; expectant time

Discussion Starters- Chapter 9

1. How do we pray for someone seriously ill? What answer do we ask for?

2. How do we know what God wants us to do for his church?

3. "Is one of you ill? He should send for the elders of the congregation to pray over him and anoint him with oil in the name of the Lord. And the prayer offered in faith will make the sick person well; the Lord will raise him from his bed, and any sins he may have committed will be forgiven." (James 5:14-15, NEB, NIV) Discuss one instance of this experienced by you or someone known to you.

4. Review 2 KEY WORDS: Renewing resources; expectant time

Share a divine message you transmitted pertaining to exact/expectant time.

10

God Ordering The Steps - And The Stops - of a Good Man: Engineering Time I

Answered needs in exact time and expectant time are most welcome. But what about answered needs in time-displaced future timeframes?

We could, of course, sulk and complain at the Lord's delay in meeting our needs. Or we could ask ourselves what the Lord is teaching us through the stops: (1) What transformation of our perspective and performance is brought about via the irritating stops? (Chapter 10); and (2) What territory must be trimmed to permit the flow of the Lord's provisions? (Chapter 11).

"They shall walk, and not faint" (Isaiah 40:31, KJV)

To faint is to lose consciousness because of insufficient blood in the brain. It is easy to visualize that mounting up with wings as eagles or even running hard demands so much more blood than the heart can pump that there is an insufficiency of blood, leading to fainting. But fainting from walking?

Provided the arteries are not blocked, why does the heart of one who is walking pump so little blood to the brain that he faints? Perhaps he is so exhausted from prolonged walking without replenishment and rest that he is experiencing what the Psalmist described so graphically: "They sickened at the sight of food and they draw near unto the gates of death." (Psalm 107:18, NEB, KJV)

Could the fainting be more a psychological condition than physical? Hiding the Israeli spies in her land from the King of Jericho, Rahab, the prostitute, says: " I know that the Lord hath given you the land, and that your terror is fallen upon us, and that all the inhabitants of the land faint because of you."(Joshua 2:9, KJV) Whether physical or psychological, fainting signifies a giving up of further effort.

"And the stops also"

In his monthly pastoral note, Dr. Robert M. Norris, senior pastor at Fourth Presbyterian Church, refers to George Mueller's comment on Psalm 37:23:

> Psalm 37:23 says: "The steps of a good man are ordered of the Lord." In the margin of his Bible, on this verse, George Mueller, that great prayer warrior and director of an orphanage, had this notation: "And the stops also." (Dr. Robert M. Norris, "Waiting for God," *The Fourth Press*, Bethesda, Md., March 1992, p. 1)

God's engineering of our circumstances

To recognize that the stops of a good man are also ordered of the Lord is to know what Dr. Richard C. Halverson, Chaplain of the United States Senate, kept repeating: "You never go anywhere by accident."He introduces Oswald Chambers's *My Utmost for His Highest*, saying, "No book except the Bible has influenced my walk with Christ at such deep and maturing levels." (Dr. Richard C. Halverson, "Introduction," in Oswald Chambers, *My Utmost for His Highest*, Discovery House, Grand Rapids, MI, p. v.)

Having been introduced to Chambers in 1945, I have been reading this marvelous daily devotional book since March 14, 1952, when I could afford my own copy. One topic of frequent reference is God's engineering of one's circumstances:

> If I do my duty, not for duty's sake, but because I believe God is engineering my circumstances, then at the very point of my obedience the whole superb grace of God is mine through the Atonement…
> We have no right to judge where we should be put, or to have preconceived notions as to what God is fitting us for. God engineers everything; wherever He puts us our one great aim is to pour out a whole-hearted devotion to Him in that particular work. "Whatsoever thy hand findeth to do, do it with thy might"…
> Whichever way God engineers circumstances, the duty is to pray. Never allow the thought – "I am of no use where I am;" because you certainly can be of no use where you are not.…
> It is only the loyal soul who believes that God engineers circumstances. We take such liberty with our circumstances, we do not believe God engineers

> them, although we say we do; we treat the things that happen as if they were engineered by men....If we learn to worship God in the trying circumstances, He will alter them in two seconds when He chooses. (Chambers, *op. cit.*, pp. 167, 114, 291, 353)

Engineering time

The stops that I know first-hand are of course, my own. In retrospect, the seven-year delay, which was half a lifetime at age 16, looks much less devastating when the delay is only the ninth of a lifetime at age 62. The key to the perspective at both ages, of course, is that God engineers my circumstances.

The timeframe is expectant time, which we defined in Chapter 2 as the future time frame of fulfillment of a divine message. However, unlike all the instances in which we found a future time of fulfillment announced at the outset, there is no such announcement in #34. We find that God engineered the circumstances (engineering time) to exceeding abundantly fulfill the rather limited hopes at the outset. Engineering time is the displaced future timeframe of fulfillment of a divine message.

Engineering Time: (1) Transformation of targets

Why can't the Lord hurry up and give me what I want-right now, if not sooner? Because He wants to transform our targets. We want just to run; He wants us to fly. We want to wade in the shallows; He wants us to dive deep.

By killing an Egyptian, Moses redressed what he thought was injustice against one Israelite. By driving him out of Egypt, training him to walk for forty years in the desert, and then bringing him back to Egypt, the Lord made him rescue 600,000 men (Exodus 12:37). Eerdman's Handbook places the total at 2,000,000 people. (David Alexander and Pat Alexander (eds.), *Eerdman's Handbook to the Bible*, Oxford, England, 1989, p.161) In other words, Moses' leadership target was transformed from one to at least 2,000,000.

Moses failed to arbitrate between just two Hebrews, but when the Lord called him up to the top of Mount Sinai (Exodus 19:20), he would give the world the most enduring set of laws; and he would be unequalled as a prophet:

> There has never yet risen in Israel a prophet like Moses, whom the LORD knew face to face – unequalled for all those miraculous signs and wonders the LORD sent him to do in Egypt, on the Pharaoh and all his servants and all his land, as well

as for all the mighty deeds and awful power which
Moses displayed in the sight of all Israel.
(Deuteronomy 34: 10-12, NEB, MOF, NIV)

Engineering Time: (2) Trimming of territory

Oswald Chambers defines the disposition of sin as my claim to my right to myself. (Chambers, *op. cit.*, p. 279) I have found time and again that the moment I deliberately gave up my claim to my right to myself, there was an astonishing and unexpected way in which a concrete need was suddenly met.The damn was broken and the torrents could flow. We'll discuss this further in Chapter 10.

#31. Answered professional need: Dream delayed for seven years – 1953 (engineering time)

In 1946, United Nations Food Agricultural Organization (FAO) held a conference in Trivandrum, Kerala, India. I was one of several assigned to assist the international delegations attending the conference. We will call *steps* those activities which facilitate the fulfillment, and *stops* the contrary ones.

Step 1: Contact with American University through delegate Clowes (1946)

The American delegate was Mr. Harry G. Clowes from the U.S. Department of Agriculture. He was sympathetic to my interest in studying in the States. He mentioned American University (AU) in Washington, D.C., and said that he knew the president. Studying in America would be a great dream!

Stop 1: Uncounseled choice of radio engineering blocked (1947)

With nobody to counsel, I thought radio engineering at AU was a good field, although I was no engineer. I have no idea why I chose radio engineering.

In a letter that Clowes sent in August, 1947, he said that he mentioned me to the AU President, and that at his request a search was made for my papers, which were found to have been delivered to the wrong person! Matters never progressed much further.

Stop 2: Engineering apparently not the indicated field of study (1947)

In the meantime, I knew I wanted to do Christ's will in choosing a career. I had been praying with and talking to Christian friends, several of whom were studying engineering, about what the Lord wanted me to do after two years of college. Toward the end of the summer, the conviction grew upon me that I was not to study engineering, even though I had good grades in the requisite fields. Engineering was the most coveted field of study because it guaranteed a job upon graduation. The engineering school was right across from our house, so if I passed the competitive entrance examination, there would be no extra expenses for room and board.

Step 2: Instead, the high-risk honors degree in economics (1947-50)

Instead of engineering, I felt I should study economics. It was considered a great step down for someone mathematically able to study economics. The state university did not even offer the subject in its curriculum. One would have to travel for 24 hours by the fastest train at great expense to another state in India which spoke a different language to study economics The tuition and room and board had to be paid in advance.

There were no textbooks or syllabus for the honors degree. You study at colleges which present you to the degree-granting university for one examination in March. Nothing done at the colleges would count toward the degree which is settled by the outcome of the written examination administered by the university.

The examinations were set by examiners in England who had no idea that the examinees had little access to current scholarly journals, no professors who kept current in their field, and no preceptors to discuss current economic issues. The examiners set the examination according to standards of Oxford or Cambridge. The examinees had to answer five out of the six essay questions presented in three hours on seven subjects, such as principles of economics, political philosophy from Plato to Marx, and every major constitution in the world. You could take the examination only once, and either you got an honors degree, converted to masters' degree in six months, or you got nothing by way of diploma for your three years of study.

To support my economics education, my father had to mortgage our rice fields. At age 43 he had to leave his native home and village, and go to a foreign country (Ceylon) in search of a business that would enable him to earn enough money to keep me in school for the next three years. There were no scholarships no student loans, no work-study programs, no public or private assistance of any kind.

Step 3: Exposure to theory of games as outside reading (1948-49)

Commission after commission have condemned the examination system as the bane of Indian education. Yet examinations not only control whether or not you graduate, but also whether you enter the coveted Indian Administrative Service. With such an overwhelming focus on examinations, neither writing term papers nor research papers were heard of in the 1940s.

Yet in 1948 I strayed far afield and read the 641-page book, *Theory of*

Games and Economic Behavior (Princeton University Press, 1947). What is more, the book so fascinated me that I felt compelled to defend it against its major detractor by writing a paper. I sent a copy of the paper to professor of economics at Princeton University, Oskar Morgenstern, co-inventor of Game Theory.

Step 4: Fellowship from Indian Statistical Institute (1950-51)

Professor Morgenstern's most generous comments ("It pleases me very much to see that the theory of games has found such an able expositor, and I hope you will be among those who will expand the work originally") were quite helpful in getting me an interview by the founding director of Indian Statistical Institute in Calcutta, three days and nights' journey by the fastest train from my home in southern India. The research and training division of the Institute selected me for a one-year immersion course in analytical statistics.

Step 5: Financial journalist – Indian Finance; Times of India (1951-53)

Advanced statistical training notwithstanding, opportunities for employment were nonexistent. A Brahmin, who would normally avoid helping a Christian, spoke to his employer whose uncle had founded *Indian Finance*. This editor created a new position for me as assistant editor of Facts & Figures, the statistical supplement that I would build up from nothing to 20% of the weekly.

In 1953, when the *Times of India* opened a new edition from Calcutta, the *Indian Finance* editor gave me his blessings to move on. He had trained me in India's foreign trade, his field of expertise. It became quite handy when I joined the *Times*. At 23, I took over the responsibility for writing on every newsworthy development in three industries: jute, tea and coal. Jute would figure in my Ph. D. dissertation

Step 6: Assistant to Professor Morgenstern at Princeton (1953)

In June 1953 I received a single page letter from Princeton offering me admission to the September session. Talk of fast turnaround! Graduate admissions to the Fall semester are announced on April 1, five months early; here I had to reply in two weeks!

Step 7: Room and board from Princeton Theological Seminary (1953-6)

There were two problems: how to pay for room and board, and how to pay for passage to the States.

Within weeks of the letter, Dr. John A. Mackay, president of Princeton Theological Seminary, was scheduled to give the commencement address at Serampore University, the only university that can even today grant theological degrees in India. Every seminary has to be affiliated with Serampore, accept its curriculum, and administer its examinations for the students to receive degrees in theology. The president of Serampore was *ex officio* senior minister of our congregation in Calcutta. He asked me if I wanted to meet Dr. Mackay. I thought he was the chairman of the department of religion, which would probably have nothing to do with economics.

When I met him, Dr. Mackay looked at the letter, and asked, "Would you want to study something else?" (I took this to mean theology.) I said, "No, economics is my first love." Dr. Mackay said, "Have Abraham (president of Serampore) write to me about you. I will take it to the dean at Princeton and tell him, 'This is what the president of the only Christian university in India has to say about the young man, and I have met him. Why don't we take him?'" Almost as an aside, he added, "We'll give you room and board." I did not know what it meant at all. I figured that it was some kind of a stipend toward living expenses.

I have already mentioned that my father's resources were strained to the utmost just to see me through college. I did not even think of asking him for any help for passage to the States. Something like five months' salary at the *Times of India* had to be raised in loans, mostly from fellow-members of the church earning less than me. A sizeable loan came from the Brahmin who sent me to his uncle for my job! None of them had any hold on me once I boarded the ship – they may have wondered if they would ever see their money again. Every penny was paid back promptly.

#32. Answered professional need: Professional contribution delayed – 1992 (engineering time)

As a professor, I am expected to make contributions to the theory and practice in my field. I consider my publications as an offering I make to the Lord for the talents He has given me, especially those of analysis and exposition. In 1972, Professor Morgenstern commented on one book, "George, you have the gift of exposition."

In 1962 I submitted a manuscript on statistics to McGraw-Hill.It seemed that they would publish it, but finally didn't. After eight or nine other rejections, a scientific and technical book publisher, American Elsevier Publishing Company, accepted it in one week, and published it in 1971. Over the years, I would submit other manuscripts to McGraw-Hill without success until 30 years later.

Technical publishing is a field in which stops seem to be the rule than steps.

In 1989, McGraw-Hill started a new series, Engineering and Technology Management Series. I presented two manuscripts for the series.

The acquisitions editor told me that my manuscripts received very strong recommendation for publishing. Of the ten manuscripts in review, mine were the top two. Imagine my shock when I received a letter from the senior editor with a flat rejection. His main point was that my book was oriented toward the business side, and not engineering.

The acquisitions editor wrote a detailed review requiring more engineering applications. I added the applications, and theory as well.The manuscript had grown 50% from its original size.

Then came a frantic call from the acquisitions editor to cut the manuscript by 100 pages. That was a most difficult thing to do because it was so tightly organized and succinctly written. But it was done.

After several months of intense work, the 416-page book was finally ready. The senior editor wrote that he was delighted to be able to enclose the first copy of *Operations Research/Management Science: Case Studies in Decision Making Under Structured Uncertainty.*

KEY WORDS: Transformation; Steps and Stops; Engineering Time

Discussion Starters – Chapter 10

1. How do we know if what we are after is what God is after?

2. Discuss: "Faith is living forward and learning backward."

3. Discuss the common features of the Steps.

4. What are common characteristics of the Stops?

5. Prayerfully share any present or recent Stops that you are experiencing.

6. Review 3 KEY WORDS: Transformation; Steps and Stops; Engineering Time

Share an experience of transformation of target in your life.

11

My Surrendering My Success Choices To His Sovereignty In Engineering Time II

Answered needs in exact time and expectant time are most welcome. But how about answered needs in time-displaced future timeframes?

We could, of course, sulk and complain at the Lord's delay in meeting our needs. Or we could ask ourselves what the Lord is teaching us through the stops: (1) What transformation of our perspective and performance is brought about via the irritating stops? (Chapter 10); and (2) What territory must be trimmed to permit the flow of the Lord's provisions? (Chapter 11).

Engineering time: (2) Trimming of territory

We referred in Chapter 9 to Oswald Chambers' definition of the disposition of sin as my claim to my right to myself. (*op. cit.*, p. 279). Notice that he does not deny "my right to myself"; it is claiming that right which makes it wrong.

Exercise God-given right to dominion

Adam and Eve were given dominion over every living creature that moved on the earth. "Be fruitful, and multiply and replenish the earth, and subdue it: and have dominion over…every living thing that moveth upon the earth." (Genesis 1:28, KJV) We further note that God wanted man to exercise his dominion, one symbol of which was the name by which he called his subjects, "Now the LORD God…brought [all the beasts of the field and all the birds of the air] to the man to see what he would name them; and whatever the man called each living creature, that was its name." (Genesis 1:19, KJV) We could picture God watching man as an earthly parent would watch his young child take possession of a pet or a toy given to him.

Surrender the finite to make room for the Infinite

If God does expect us to exercise our God-given dominion as good stewards, we can see how God would transform our targets, enlarging them and endowing them with fulfillment above and beyond our wildest dreams. But why do we have to trim our territory?

To trim (hair, a hedge) is to make it neat by clipping; to trim sails is to adjust sails for sailing. God gave us dominion over the abilities and resources He has given us. He wants us to offer them up to Him, acknowledging and accepting His infinite control over our finite abilities and resources. We must manage what He has sent our way to the best of our abilities. After doing our utmost, we say: Lord, here is my utmost; please use them for Your highest.

The late Professor Dr. V. K Alexander of Union Christian College, Kerala, India, used to say that we are like arrows in God's hand. As we are stretched and stretched, we complain of the strain; but the Archer knows where He is aiming us. Trimming our territory is a conscious and deliberate offering of our tension to reach His targets, which we cannot see. I hope that these instances where I felt the sustained pressure would be used by the Lord to show you the tensions He is putting you through to reach the targets beyond your horizons to achieve His highest.

#33. Answered spiritual need: Surrendering my right to define my intellectual profession – 1943 (engineering time)

At age 13, I was a high school junior in India. The school year starts in June, while the colleges open later. A team of college students, including a medical student, descended on the school. They talked to us in groups and one-on-one about personal acceptance of Jesus Christ as Lord and Savior.

We were all members of Mar Thoma Syrian Church. The church is believed to have been founded in Kerala, India, in A.D. 52 by Thomas, the doubting disciple of Jesus Christ. Those of us "born on the walls of the church," wore our badge of ancient origins with pride, but were never challenged to make a personal confession, in spite of mandatory Sunday school through age 16.

Thus, the descent of the team of College kids shook things up. I remember asking about collecting food for the poor, but the medical student saw through it and said that the pressing question was personal acceptance of Christ. By all counts, I was a "good" boy, a role model. Medicine was both prestigious and paying. I had not thought of medical school – too far down the line. But I knew I had brains, and felt that I should be a good steward of that talent.

I had a major concern. If I gave my life to the Lord, what if He chose me to be a minister? Even today, the nominal salaries of ministers are rarely paid regularly by the congregations, because the "cashless" society simply does not have the cash to pay the salaries. While they cannot count on regular income, they are required to set an example by wearing spotless, white cloaks. The cloaks easily get soiled and dirty in the dusty rural lanes and beaten paths; and soap is expensive. So, the wives of ministers have to do the laundry daily, patiently beating the dirt out of the cloaks, soaking them in primitive substitutes for bleaching powder, hanging them out to dry in the sun, starching them and ironing them for use the next day or the day after.

Someone entering the ministry must feel such a compelling need to preach the Gospel – "I can do no other" – that he would take what amounts to a *de facto* vow of poverty, not only for himself, but also for his children.

Looking around, I couldn't find any clergyman whose intelligence overwhelmed me. On the contrary, the sermons were insipid and uninspiring. At 13, I couldn't help thinking: "Me a minister? What a waste it would be!" But I dared not say it aloud for fear that my worst fears could come true.

But I struggled with the question of letting the Lord take over my life. Slowly I acknowledged that the Lord, who gave me the brains, knew best what to do with them. That meant that He could call me to the ministry. Nobody told me that a call to the ministry was not inevitable. Finally, I came to accept the thought that I would go where the Lord sent me, even into the ministry.

I recall silently making the commitment just before the 8 P.M.. Study time at the small school dormitory which housed a dozen kids from villages beyond walking distance. I felt a sense of great peace. The evangelistic team arranged for the new crop of born-again Christians to give our testimony at nearby churches. The older folk "born on the walls of the church" seemed to take it in stride, and even encouraged some of us.

What was the trimming of territory involved in the personal acceptance of Christ? What I learned was that I submit my God-given dominion over my talents to God's dominion without knowing ahead what He would do with them. That hard choice would come in four years when, as previously discussed, I was led to studying the virtually unknown field of economics over the objections of friends and family, who thought I should use my mathematical abilities and study engineering.

#34. Answered professional need: Surrendering my right to a passport – 1953 (engineering time)

We saw in #31. Answered professional need that I had only two months to arrange passage and raise money for passage, as well as to resolve the larger issue of funds for room and board in Princeton. There was another problem which threatened to void everything else: getting a passport.

I applied for the passport in Calcutta, and expected it to be issued in a week or two. But there seemed to be some problems. I tried to resolve them, but each successive higher level authority said that it could not issue a passport because I was from out of town. Prospects of going to Princeton seemed more and more remote with each turndown.

The last person said that I could see the Secretary, the highest official. I went in to see him. He said that he needed a report from the police of my home state before he could issue my passport. Any inquiry sent by slow mail from one state to another would take several days. Even if all communications went post-haste, Calcutta would not have a police report before six weeks, a full month after the ship would have sailed.

I remember sitting in front of the Secretary, and seeing my dream of going to Princeton evaporate into thin air. I remember feeling calm. "If the Lord doesn't want me to go to Princeton, so be it," I said to myself. All human avenues seemed closed.

The very next moment, the Secretary noticed from my application that I had gone out of the country to Ceylon (now Sri Lanka) three years ago. He asked, "You got a pass to go to Ceylon?" "Yes, from Madras," I replied (which was not my state, but my state of residence at that time). He said, "Since your state issued you a pass, we can use that as the basis of a police clearance. You can have your passport tomorrow."

After all my earnest and painstaking efforts, I surrendered my right to define success in my own terms and told the Lord, "Have it your way, Lord." And He did. Chambers says, "If we learn to worship God in the trying circumstances, He will alter them in two seconds when He chooses." (*op. cit.*, p. 353)

KEY WORDS:Trimming my territory; my claim to my right to myself; engineering time

Discussion Starters – Chapter 11

1. Prayerfully share instances which you experienced delayed fulfillments.

2. Discuss: "Faith is living forward and learning backward." (*Interceding with the Infinite*, p.156.)

3. Discuss the common features of the steps in this chapter.

4. What are common characteristics of the stops in this chapter?

5."If we learn to worship God in the trying circumstances, He will alter them in two seconds when He chooses" – Oswald Chambers. Discuss.

6. Review 3 KEY WORDS: Trimming my territory; my claim to my right to myself; engineering time

Share an experience of trimming of territory in your life.

12

DISCO (1): Discerning the Demand

The practice of prayer power is discussed under two acronyms DISCO (Chs. 12-14), and LISCO (Chs. 15-17). In chapter 1, I combined DISCO and LISCO under one acronym DEAVECO. Splitting it into two seems to facilitate practicing prayer power.

We do not rush in where we see a need, but await the guidance of the Spirit to discern the demand, claim a promise, and access our own resources. We listen to the Lord, communicate the message He gives us, and offer thanks for His provisions.

"Who touched me?"

Jesus healed a lunatic from the tombs who could not be controlled because he broke every fetter. The severity of his affliction is reflected in his answer to Jesus' question, "What is your name? " "Legion," he said, "there is a host of us." (Mark 5:9, MOF)

Enlarging crowds

The man went off and spread the news in the Ten Towns of all that Jesus had done for him, (Mark 5:20, NEB) which must have swelled the size of the crowd. "A great crowd once more gathered round him." (Mark 5:21, NEB) Next comes the president of one of the synagogues, Jairus, who throws himself at Jesus' feet and says, "I beg you to come and lay your hands on [my little daughter (who) is at death's door] and save her life." (Mark 5:24, NEB) Jesus goes with him. And the crowd is growing even larger because of the expectation of Jesus either saving or failing to save the daughter of a synagogue president from death. "A large crowd followed and pressed around him." (Mark 5:25, NIV)

One single need

We now zero in on a single woman in that large crowd that is pressing upon Jesus. She has suffered from hemorrhages for twelve years. In spite of long treatment by many doctors, costing her all her money, there had been no improvement; on the contrary, she had grown worse.

She hears excited talk about the miracles of Jesus. She hesitates. According to the New English Bible, she comes up "from behind in the crowd."(Mark 5:27) The New International Version has her coming up "behind him in the crowd." Of course, she could have come from behind in the crowd, and then reached out to Jesus from behind him. She is telling herself, "If I just touch his clothes, I will be healed." (Mark 5:28, NIV) She reaches out and barely touches Jesus' cloak. "Immediately her bleeding stopped and she felt in her body that she was freed from her suffering." (Mark 5:27, NIV)

Demand for resources and instantaneous fulfillment

That touch reached out for resources – concrete resources for specific needs. To touch she had to hope; and hope was what she did not have. Every time she went to a new doctor, she was hoping, "This time, I will be healed." But every time she was disappointed. And she had no resources to pay more doctors' bills. Yet, when she heard about Jesus, she says, "If I just touch his clothes, I will be healed."

Moffatt's translation says, "Jesus was at once conscious that some healing virtue had passed from him." (Mark 5:30) The New International Version refers to "power": " At once Jesus realized that power had gone out from him." Phillips points out the dramatic impact of the touch. Jesus feels the power that went out, and he halts the crowd in its onward movement: "At once Jesus knew intuitively that power had gone out of him, and he turned round in the middle of the crowd and said, 'Who touched my clothes?'" (Mark 5: 30, PHI)

The disciples are puzzled by Jesus' question. When scores of people are pressing on Jesus at any given moment, how can any single person be identified? Notice that the woman could indeed understand the significance of Jesus' question: "Whose touch drew the power of healing from me?" His disciples replied, "You can see this crowd jostling you. How can you ask, 'Who touched me?'" But he looked all around at their faces to see who had done so. Then the woman, scared and shaking, came and flung herself before him and told him the whole story. But he said to her, "Daughter, it is your faith that has healed you. Go home in peace, and be free from your trouble." (Mark 5:31-34, PHI)

Rejection of many needy cases

Most probably, in that crowd of thousands, she was not the only one who needed physical healing for a pressing ailment. There were very few doctors, and they were expensive. All sorts of illness and ailments were commonplace. In that crowd of say, 5,000 people, there were easily 500 serious cases of ailments. Yet only *one* was healed. Why that one, and no other? What does she have that 499 other sick men and women did not?

Jesus drew sharp fire from the congregation when he told them in the synagogue that God rejected Israel's specific needs. Elijah bypassed *all* the needy widows in Israel; and Elisha bypassed *all* the needy lepers in Israel. To add insult to injury, foreigners whom Israel looked down on were selected to be given concrete resources for specific needs: renewing resources for sustenance for the widow of Zarephath through Elijah, and recompensing resources for healing for Naaman through Elisha. He said:

> I tell you the plain fact that in Elijah's time, when the heavens were shut up for three and a half years and there was a great famine through the whole country, there were many widows in Israel, but Elijah was not sent to any of them. But he was sent to Sarepta [Zarephath], to a widow in the country of Sidon. In the time of Elisha the prophet, there were many lepers in Israel, but not one of them was healed - only Naaman, the Syrian. (Luke 5:25-27, MOF, PHI)

Discerning the need: (1) The need one's absolute assurance of the unseen

The woman with the hemorrhage unquestioningly believed Jesus would heal her, something which none of her doctors could do for twelve years.

Similarly, the widow of Zarephath believed unquestioningly in God's promise: "For this is what the LORD, the God of Israel, says: 'The jar of flour will not be used up and the jug of oil will not run dry until the day the LORD gives rain on the land.'" (1 King 17:14, NIV)

Notice that the God of Israel is foreign to the widow from Sidon. Further, the God is an unknown God. She may even know that it is the same God who has spoken through Elijah, who is at that very same time holding back the rain from the land. Yet, when he asks, she gives up half of her worldly possessions to feed the stranger.

The theme is the same in the case of Naaman. It is his foreign maid that tells her mistress, "If only my master would see the prophet who is in Samaria! He would cure him of his leprosy." (2 Kings 5:3, NIV)

All the three instances shared absolute assurance of the unseen. The unseen was utterly impossible: stopping of hemorrhage that no doctor could cure in twelve years; perpetually replenishing flour and oil every day for two years; healing of dreaded leprosy for which there was no known cure. Yet, in each instance, the one in need of concrete resources had to act as though he or she had already received what was being requested.

Discerning the need: (2) The intercessor's specific commissioning

Which need shall we intercede for? That need for which we are sent.

Elijah was sent to the widow of Zarephath. Elisha was sent to Naaman, not physically and directly, but just as though he were. Elisha heard of the king of Israel tearing his robes when Naaman was sent to him by the king of Syria asking that Naaman be cured of his leprosy. Jesus was sent to the woman with the hemorrhage, the touching of his clothes by her being her claim of a promise.

Discerning the need: (3) Supportive community's recommendation

What led to the woman with the hemorrhage to reach out to touch Jesus' robes? All her experience to date had been negative. She went to many learned physicians; she underwent many expensive treatments, each one with renewed expectation of a favorable answer. However, every time she was completely disappointed.

The testimony of the anonymous community – passive intercession

Here is a crowd talking excitedly about a prophet, a holy man. She hears stories of the miracles of Jesus. The anonymous crowd recommends Jesus to her, unaware that they are indeed bearing witness to Jesus. Perhaps two or three around her in that huge crowd sparks in her a renewed hope of healing, thereby becoming an anonymous community of believers. That part of the crowd recommends Jesus to her; and she accepts.

The commendation of the neighboring community – active intercession

The reverse side of the recommendation is seen in the case of the Roman centurion. Instead of recommending Jesus to the intercessee, the woman with hemorrhage, the crowd recommends the intercessee to Jesus.

Interestingly, the one with the faith is again the foreigner. He figures that the Jewish elders can put in a good word for him, an army captain of the occupying power of Rome. His slave, whom he thinks highly of, is seriously ill and in fact at the point of death. "[H]e sent some Jewish elders to him with his request that [Jesus] would come and save his slave's life. When they came to Jesus, they urged him strongly to grant his request, saying: 'He deserves to have this favor from you. He loves our nation and has built us a synagogue out of his own pocket.'" (Luke 7:3-5, PHI, MOF)

The Jewish leaders must themselves be open to Jesus. They are asking him to save a dying man, and are confident that Jesus can indeed accomplish the miracle. That faith in Jesus is most unpopular with the Jewish establishment, making it a dangerous stand for Jewish elders to take. Yet, they not only affirm their faith in Jesus, but also commend a most unusual foreigner, part and parcel of the foreign establishment which rules over Israel with an iron hand. But he builds them a synagogue out of his own pocket, generously contributing to support a foreign religion.

The upholding action of the friendly community – active intercession

Again in Capernaum, we see another type of commendation by the community. Instead of the words of the Jewish leaders, we have the action of four friends. Finding that the paralytic whom they wanted Jesus to heal could not be brought into the house, they take a dramatic step. They place their petition for someone else – intercession – before Jesus. "[They] removed the tiles from the roof over Jesus' head and let down the paralytic's bed through the opening. And when Jesus saw their faith, he said to the man who was paralyzed, "My son, your sins are forgiven." (Mark 2:4-5, PHI)

Discerning the need: (4) Identified role in intercession

The mighty ministry of intercession – of bearing one another's burdens, thus fulfilling the law of Christ – is a mystery.

Human role in Divine intercession

It is God who asks us to intercede; it is through Christ (God) that we pray; and it is the Holy Ghost (God) who intercedes with groanings that defy utterance. If intercession is thus initiated by God, implored through God, and implemented by God, then are we totally superfluous? No, we are the medium through which the particular intercession is accomplished at each particular time and place.

Active and passive roles

Abram interceded actively for Abimelech; so did Ananias for Saul.

The Jewish leaders interceded for the Roman army captain's slave. Since they spoke to Jesus, we would call that *active intercession.*

The four friends who raised the roof to bring to Jesus the paralytic did not say anything, but their actions spoke louder than words, so that Jesus commended their faith: active intercession.

How about the people who were closest to the woman with the hemorrhage? Quite possibly, they had no idea that the woman was so ill, and that she had spent all her money on doctors. Yet, it is their excited discussion of Jesus' miracles that led her to find faith and edge toward Jesus. That testimony was *passive intercession.*

Discerning the need: (5) Sources of requests for intercession

The air around is filled with radio waves. We do not hear them, unless and until we have a receiver and we are on the right wavelength.

God's direct initiative

God asks Abimelech to ask Abraham to intercede for him. God asks Ananias to intercede for Saul. In the first instance, God initiates intercession with the one for whom intercession is offered (intercessee). In the second instance, God initiates intercession with the one who intercedes (intercessor).

God's indirect initiative – Through concerned people

The four friends who carried the paralytic interceded for him. God gave them the faith and the will to act on that faith.

God's blocking of concerned people's initiative

However, despite the best intentions of the concerned people, intercession could be ineffective if the intercessee has no receptivity. In the story of Lazarus, who begged at the gate of the rich man, the poor man dies and goes to heaven and the rich man to Hades.

As he is being tortured in Hades, he sees Lazarus in Abraham's bosom, and asks to send Lazarus "to dip his finger-tip in water and cool my tongue, for I am in anguish in these flames." Abraham says that there is a great gulf between us and you to keep back traffic in both directions." Then he said, 'Well father, I beg you to send him to my father's house, for I have five brothers: let him bear testimony to them, that they may not come to this place of torture as well.'" (Luke 16: 27-28, MOF)

Abraham points out that the five brothers have Moses and the prophets, but the rich man pleads: "'No, father Abraham,' he said, 'but if someone only goes to them from the dead, they will repent.' He said to him, 'If they will not listen to Moses and the prophets, they will not be convinced, not even if one rose from the dead.'" (Luke 16:30-31, MOF)

The rich man was genuinely concerned about his five brothers on earth. However, his pleas in behalf of them were not granted because the brothers were apparently not receptive to the resources: repentance.

Is this intercession really necessary?

What particular need am I sent to intercede for right now? The existence of a need, or our awareness of it, by itself, does not constitute the command that we intercede for it. We are here referring to intercession for concrete resources to meet specific needs such as "Joe's" reassignment, "Joan's" reemployment.

Criterion 1: Does the Spirit move you?

Since it is the Holy Ghost who must intercede with groanings that defy utterance, the prime test is: Does the Spirit indwelling in me recognize this situation as requiring my intercession right now?

We see that Jesus was "moved": "As he saw the crowds he was moved with pity for them; they were harassed and dejected, like sheep without a shepherd. Then he said to his disciples, "The harvest is rich, but the laborers are few; so pray the Lord of the harvest to send laborers to gather his harvest." (Matthew 9:36-38, MOF)

Note that the richness of the harvest does not mean that I am the one to reap this particular portion of the harvest at this time. I must "pray the Lord of the harvest to send laborers" (including me) to gather the Lord's harvest.

Criterion 2: Do you discern God's interests?

Given that you are led to intercede, what is your objective? It is only too easy to say, "My will be done," asking the Lord to give a blank check to meet your demands. Instead, am I prepared to say, "Thy will be done," and mean it?

None of this is to suggest that we should suppress our warmth, ignore our eagerness to see our fondest wishes for the intercessory situation to come true, and offer emaciated, nampy-pampy mutterings about "Whatever will be, will be: *Que sera, sera.*"

Criterion 3: Do you intercede with all your might?

On the contrary, you are the appointed advocate for the intercessee. You have every right to ask the Lord for concrete resources to meet his or her specific needs. An advocate argues for his client; so do I as an intercessor. However, much as I share my intercessee's petition, I have to hold myself willing to the Lord's overruling of it. Give it all you've got; and then let God answer in His own way, far above what we can dare hope for. Moses shows the extreme extent of identification of the advocate with the client. He asked the Lord to blot his name out of the book of life:

> The next day Moses said to the people: "You have committed a great sin. I shall now go up to the LORD; perhaps I may be able to secure pardon for your sin." So Moses returned to the LORD and said, "O hear me! This people has committed a great sin: they have made themselves gods of gold. If thou wilt forgive them, forgive. But if not, blot out my name, I pray , from thy book which thou hast written." (Exodus 32:30-32, NEB)

Discern the need; claim the promise

Receive the burden of intercession when the Lord lays it on you; don't rush into it. When sent by the Lord of the harvest, He will give you all the necessary resources; so also, when the Lord asks you to intercede for someone, He will give you the promise to claim which will bring you the concrete resources for the specific needs, as we will discuss in the next chapter.

> KEY WORDS: Discerning The demand; active intercession; passive intercession

Discussion Starters – Chapter 12

1. How do you find out in practice the answer to the question: Is this intercession really necessary?

2. How did those outside of Israel qualify for answers to concrete needs?

3."At once Jesus realized that power had gone out from him." Recount an experience in which you felt the Lord's power which opened paths which were closed.

4. Share a specific need for which you interceded with all your might, and received the answer: (1) in the affirmative; and (2) in the negative.

5. "If only you had been here, Lord," said Martha, "my brother would never have died, And I know that, even now, God will give you whatever you ask from him." (John 11: 21-22, PHI) How well do we recognize this expectations of our intercession? How do we discharge it?

6. Review 3 KEY WORDS: Discerning The demand; active intercession; passive intercession

Share an impulse to intercede that you obeyed which brought a blessing.

13

DISCO (2): Claiming The Promise

The practice of prayer power is discussed under two acronyms DISCO (Chs. 12-14), and LISCO (Chs. 15-17). We do not rush in where we see a need, but await the guidance of the Spirit to <u>dis</u>cern the demand, <u>c</u>laim a promise, and access our <u>o</u>wn resources. We <u>lis</u>ten to the Lord, <u>c</u>ommunicate the message He gives us, and <u>o</u>ffer thanks for His provisions.

"I will surely deliver thee" (Jeremiah 39:18, KJV)
"But if not" (Daniel 3:18, KJV)

In 607 B.C. King Nebuchadnezzar of Babylon overran Jerusalem, and brought home not only the vessels from the temple, but also "Young men without any physical defect, handsome, showing aptitude for every kind of learning, well informed, quick to understand, and qualified to serve in the king's palace," (Daniel 1:4, NIV) The chief among them were Daniel (renamed Belteshazzar), Hananiah (renamed Shadrach), Mishael (Meshach) and Azariah (Abednego), the latter being administrators over the province under Daniel, its ruler.

Obeying God at the cost of imminent fiery death

Four years later, the king makes a golden image 90 feet high and 9 feet broad, as tall as 15 men, or a 5-story building. A most impressive and expensive a structure! And the king commands everyone to fall down and worship the golden image he had set up, at the sound of horn, flute, zither, lyre, pipe, and all kinds of music. Obeying the first of the Ten Commandments, Daniel and friends refuse to fall down and worship the image. The astrologers were bested by Daniel by telling the king his dream that he couldn't recall. Daniel also interpreted it, causing the astrologers to complain to the king that the foreign administrators over Babylon are neither serving the king's gods nor worshipping his golden image.

The incredulous king summons his favorite administrators and offers another chance for them to redeem themselves by worshipping at the next signal. They replied, "O Nebuchadnezzar, we do not need to defend ourselves before you in this matter. If we are thrown into the blazing furnace, the God we serve is able to save us from it, and he will rescue us from your hand, O king. But if not, we want you to know, O king, that we will not serve your gods or worship the image of gold you have set up)." (Daniel 3:18, NIV, KJV)

Claimable promise

God is able to save us, Daniel and company say. But if God chooses not to, still we will serve Him, and will not worship the golden image. There is no question of God's power to save them; and facing imminent death in the fiery furnace, made seven times as hot as normal, they would not be human if they did not claim God's promise: "For I will surely deliver thee (I will certainly rescue you), and thou shalt not fall by the sword, but thy life shall be for a prey unto thee (but will escape with your life); because thou hast put thy trust in me, saith the LORD." (Jeremiah 39:18, KJV, MOF, NIV) While invoking the promise to preserve their lives, they trust God even if they do not survive.

May I briefly recall what I said in Chapter 1 to make sure that we do not take the Scripture in vain. It is not our wisdom that chooses an appropriate Scripture, but the Lord's gift to the intercessory situation.

Affirmative answer: Rescued not from, but *in* the fire

God does not keep Daniel and friends from the fire; He saves them in the fire. Nebuchadnezzar is incredulous to see the three whom his strongest soldiers threw into the blazing furnace walking free: "Lo, I see four men loose, walking in the midst of the fire, and they have no hurt; and the form of the fourth is like the Son of God."(Daniel 3:25, KJV)

"May this cup be taken from me... yet not as I will, but as thou wilt" (Matthew 26:39, NIV, KJV)

From this event that was answered in the affirmative, we turn to an event answered in the negative in the New Testament.

We see Jesus in the Garden of Gethsemene, agonizing over the crucifixion. Any man would want to escape the cruelest of all deaths, that upon the cross. Yet, God's justice will not be met without the punishment of sin upon the cross. The agony of Jesus was so intense that an angel appeared to strengthen him as narrated by Luke: "And being in agony he prayed more earnestly: and his sweat was as it were great drops of blood falling down to the ground...And there appeared an angel unto him from heaven, strengthening him." (Luke 22:44,43, KJV)

Claimable promise

If there were no agony, there would be no need to deliberately choose God's will in the matter of Jesus' crucifixion. "Father, if it be thy will, take this cup from me. Yet not my will but thine be done." (Luke 22:42, NEB) Facing imminent death on the cross, Christ could well have claimed the promise that Daniel and friends could have claimed, "For I will certainly rescue you, and thou shalt not fall by the sword, but will escape with your life; because thou hast put thy trust in me, saith the LORD."

Negative answer – "Became obedient to death – even death on a Cross! (Philippians 2:8, NIV)

While Daniel and company were spared from death, Christ was not: "This was why I came into the world." (John 18:37, MOF) The death on the cross was not because of a failed plan; it *was* the plan. God's interaction in human history would demand the cross, so that through Christ's resurrection mankind may receive life eternal. However, from the human viewpoint, the promise Christ could have claimed in his agony in Gethsemene – to let the cup of Crucifixion and death pass from him – was answered in the negative.

General promise: "Whatever you ask... All your needs"

The focus of prayer, in both the Old and the New Testament, is surviving imminent death. However, unlike Daniel in the Old Testament, and Jesus Christ in the New Testament, we pray most often for less traumatic issues of life than of death.

Basis for our intercession

We intercede for others because He intercedes in our behalf. "And if any man sin, we have an advocate with the Father, Jesus Christ the righteous (one who speaks to the Father in our defense)" (1 John 2:1, KJV, NIV) He also interceded while on earth, "Oh, Simon, Simon, do you know that Satan has claimed the right to sift you all like wheat, but I have prayed for you, Simon, that you may not lose your own faith." (Luke 22:31-32, PHI, MOF, NIV) What does an advocate do? An advocate pleads the cause of another by argument. In a court of law, the advocate would muster the arguments most favorable to the defendant, and then cite the laws that provide him with the least punishment. The object of the argument is to establish that the cited laws are indeed the appropriate laws applicable to the particular case.

What is the "argument" that our intercessor brings forth? Not the merits of the intercessee, but the unmerited grace. What is applicable "law?" In my name:

> And I will do whatever you ask in my name, so that

> the Son may bring glory to the Father. You may ask me for anything in my name, and I will do it." (John 14:13-14, NIV) "And my God will meet all your needs according to his glorious riches in Christ Jesus." (Philippians 4:19, NIV)

In my name

The ground upon which we make our requests is "In My Name." That has the prefix: "If it be thy will." The prefix acknowledges that we do not know what is best for us, limited as we are by time and space, but that our heavenly Father does know. "Align us with thy will," is our prayer. As Jesus did, we ask God to meet our concrete needs, deliberately subjecting our own success choices to His sovereignty. From the general promise, let us turn to specific promises.

Specific promises: (1) Financial needs

How do we invoke the promise that applies to our specific need? It has to be provided by the Lord. As we seek His guidance on the promise to be claimed, He may bring to our memory a particular incident in the Scripture, a particular verse. Or, given an area in the Scripture, we may diligently search until we find the particular verse. We share some of the verses which we were given at Taipei International Church:

Matthew 6:11 (KJV)

Our Father, who taught us to pray, "Give us this day our daily bread," and thereby sanctified the material needs of our daily life, we pray for Jane's brother who needs money for the downpayment for a car, and for Cecilia's friend who needs money for his child's operation in Taipei. (April 15, 1984)

Matthew 6:11 (KJV)

Oh Thou who taught us to pray, saying, "Give us this day our daily bread," grant us the faith of Apostle Paul: "My God will supply all your own needs from His glorious resources in Christ Jesus," we pray for Albert's father in New Jersey who needs a job right now, Jane's mother in Taipei who needs a part-time job, and the college student who desperately needs summer work, not only to continue his studies, but also to continue the healing of the wounds from past summers at home in the United States. (March 11, 1984)

Mark 2:4 (MOF)

Oh Lord, who commended the faith of the four who lowered the pallet on which the paralytic lay, we would lift up 14-year-old Chiang Lan-Yu from Orchid Island in her surgical bed as she undergoes staging operation for Hodgkins' Disease tomorrow. We pray with Connie Jordan for wisdom for the doctors and finances for the treatment. (April 15, 1984)

The reason I included the last intercession is because I had in my file a Special Offering envelope which said: (NT $1000 for the brother / sister who needs money for medical surgery as mentioned in the intercessory prayer on April 15, 1984)." While the money was passed on to Connie Jordan, the missionary working with aboriginal children, the envelope with its inscription is kept in my intercession file as an identified answer.

Specific promises: (2) Physical needs

The last item was included under physical needs because the primary need was physical. Here are additional instances of promises claimed for healing:

Mark 1:34 (RSV)

Oh Jesus Christ, who "healed many who were sick with various diseases," we pray for Warren Graham's 90-year-old mother who is on the critical list after a heart attack in Valdosta, Georgia. Place thy healing hand over her; comfort her, and restore her to health, oh Lord, we pray. We would now pray that Thou would heal the one with cardiac arrhythmia. Restore unto Thy servant wholeness of body so that it be a joyous witness to Thy glory, we pray. (March 4, 1984)

Matthew 4:23 (MOF)

Oh Christ, who "made a tour through the whole of Galilee,...healing all sickness and disease among the people," we pray with the wife whose husband is recovering from the auto accident. We pray for the one suffering from backache due to the slipped disc, as well as her friend who has heart trouble. Stretch out Thy healing hand over each one, Oh Lord, and restore them to wholeness of body and spirit, we pray. (March 11, 1984)

Mark 5:41 (MOF)

Oh Thou who art the healer of mind, body, and spirit, who conquered even death when Thou commanded Jairus' 12-year-old daughter, "Little girl, rise, I tell you," we raise to Thee 14-year-old Chang Lan-Yu, whom Connie Jordan is seeing through cobalt therapy for Hodgkins' Disease. May she touch the hem of Thy garment! We petition Thee with Michele for her mother's healing without surgery. (March 25, 1984)

Jeremiah 9:18 (MOF)

Oh Lord who spoke through Jeremiah, "I will certainly rescue you," we thank Thee for plucking him out of the jaws of death in the serious automobile accident in Bangkok, Ted Skiles who escaped with 21 stitches on his head, and for enabling him to go home after the hospital. We pray for his full recovery to resume his ministry with his wife for the orphans at the Home of God's Love that we remember in our special offering today. (April 29, 1984)

Specific promises: (3) Professional needs

Romans 10:15 (KJV)

Remind us, Our Father, to exclaim with Paul, "How beautiful are the feet of them that preach the gospel of peace," and offer Thee high praise and hearty thanksgiving for Thy servant Mike to whom Thou hast granted the gift of healing hearts by grace. Even as Thou guided Abram from the known and the familiar to the unknown and the unfamiliar in fulfillment of Thy great purpose, show Mike where and when he should serve Thee, Oh Lord. (October 21, 1984)

John 5:30 (KJV)

Oh Christ who declared, "I seek not mine own will, but the will of the Father which hath sent me," we pray for Thy daughter who seeks to do Thy will, asking that Thou would make clear to her what she should do for Thee. (March 18, 1984)

Psalm 147:7 (KJV)

Oh Lord, grant us the grace to "Sing unto [Thee] with thanksgiving" as the Psalmist urges us to do, especially for showing Thy will to the one who sought it, so that she now enjoys peace and the joy of professional fulfillment. (October 21, 1984)

We pray for the Carltons who seek Thy will to respond this week to the call from Tel Aviv, Israel, to serve there next year, not knowing where Thou wants them to serve Thee next year – in Vienna, Tokyo, Singapore, or elsewhere. Guide Prudence to enter the seminary Thou hast chosen for her preparation to become a missionary. Grant each one of them, Oh Lord, the joy of knowing that they do Thy will. (March 11, 1984)

We give Thee hearty thanks for three identified answers. We thank Thee for the specific guidance Thou hast given the Carltons in showing them that Thou hast called them be Thy witnesses in Tel Aviv. We thank Thee for the improvement in the diabetic condition of Caryl Struhke's mother in Wilmington, Delaware, and for the progressive recovery from the serious automobile accident that Thou art providing Thy servant in the United States. (March 25, 1984)

James 1:17 (KJV)

Oh God from whom cometh "every good and every perfect gift," we thank Thee for the Chinese young man who left Tuesday to pursue Ph.

D. work in Florida, and ask that his dedicated preparation will enable him to offer Thee acceptable fruits of accomplishment. (March 25, 1984)

Specific needs: (4) Relational needs

Psalm 42:1 (KJV)

Oh Lord, the yearning for Whom is described by the Psalmist "as the hart [panting] after the water brooks," we pray that the one who feels estranged from Thee and family may see the eager outreach of Thy Fatherly love in and through his earthly family, and come home to Thee and to them. (April 29, 1984)

Ezekiel 11:17 (MOF)

Oh God, Who art the author of peace and lover of concord, we claim Thy promise made through Ezekiel: "I will give them a new nature and put a new spirit into them" for specific individuals and families: patience and peace for Thy son who yearns to experience Thy love; assurance and affirmation for Thy son who is struggling with the idea of Christian community as a means of grace; the grace to give and forgive for Thy couples who may know afresh Thy unconditional acceptance of them; and comfort and courage for the mother who, for the sake of a better future for her children, had to recently accept long-term separation from them. Anoint them each with thy holy unction, Oh Lord! (Oct. 21, 1984)

John 21:16 (MOF)

Oh Christ, who when Thou asked, "Simon, son of John, do you love me?" knew already Simon Peter's love for his Lord, we uplift the families agonizing over their covenants to one another so that they too may rediscover their love in Thee (April 15, 1984)

Specific promises: (5) Spiritual needs

Matthew 6:9 (KJV)

Oh Lord, who taught us to pray "Our Father," thereby sanctifying the bonds of family, we uphold the one who is earnestly praying that his father in the States be touched and freed by Thee; and we pray for Jerry's rebirth in Christ. (March 25, 1984)

Romans 10:15 (KJV)

Recalling with Paul, "How beautiful are the feet of them that preach the gospel of peace!," we lift to Thy throne of grace Doris Brougham and each member of Heavenly Melody Singers as they sing Thy message in troubled Northern Island as well as in Great Britain. (March 18, 1984)

Luke 11:9, 13 (RSV)

Oh Lord, who hath promised: "Ask, and it will be given you," and emphasized: "How much more will the heavenly Father give the Holy

Spirit to those who ask him!" we uplift three different families praying earnestly for specific loved ones to know Thee as Lord and Savior: the wife in Cape Town, South Africa; the two grown children in the United States; and the aunt and family in Taipei. Make them one in Thee, Oh Lord, so that they may know the joy of being a family in Christ! (March 11, 1984)

Ephesians 1:18 (KJV)
We thank Thee for Franz's son who wants to enter Bible school in September in Ontario, Canada. Thou knowest the father's opposition to the son's schooling. Open Franz's "eyes of understanding" to Thy salvation, to the glory of Thy name, we pray. (Mar 4, 1993)

Psalm 9:1 (KJV)
As the Psalmist sang, "I will praise Thee, Oh Lord, with my whole heart; I will show forth all thy marvelous works," we praise Thee now especially for three identified answers to our prayers here: for the astounding recovery from spinal surgery that Thou hast granted Taipei American School student Junior Kauffman, who has been able to walk in his hospital room; for the offer of help to Franz's son preparing to enter Bible college in September, now with the approval and support of his father; and for the glory to Thy name that Doris Brougham and the Heavenly Melody Singers have been able to bring in England as recounted in her warm letter to the editor of *The China Post* from Ipswich. (April 29, 1984)

KEY WORDS:In My Name; But if not; advocate.

Discussion Starters – Chapter 13

1. How do you avoid haphazard selections like: Matt 27:5 and Luke 10:37?

2. "For I will surely deliver thee (I will certainly rescue you), and thou shalt not fall by the sword, but thy life shall be for a prey unto thee (but will escape with your life); because thou hast put thy trust in me, saith the LORD." How would you apply this promise to a dying person?

3. Are we presenting an ultimatum to God when claiming a promise? Why should we claim a promise when praying for a concrete need?

4. Share a specific need in the financial and physical categories for

which you claimed a promise and received an affirmative answer.

5. Share a specific need in the professional, relational, and spiritual categories for which you claimed a promise and received an affirmative answer.

6. Review 3 KEY WORDS: In My Name; But if not; advocate.

Share a concrete need for which you claimed a promise, and received an answer in the negative.

14

DISCO (3): Accessing Own Resources

The practice of prayer power is discussed under two acronyms DISCO (Chs. 11-13), and LISCO (Chs. 14-16). We do not rush in where we see a need, but await the guidance of the Spirit to discern the demand, claim a promise, and access our own resources. We listen to the Lord, communicate the message He gives us, and offer thanks for His provisions.

"The Lord needs them" (Matthew 21:3, PHI)

It is springtime. To celebrate Passover, the great feast marking Israel's liberation from Egypt, the people crowd into Jerusalem from near and far. Jesus stays at the home of Lazarus in Bethany, two miles from Jerusalem. As he reaches Bethpage, the halfway point, he sends two disciples to fetch him a donkey and her colt: "Untie them and bring them to me. If anyone says anything to you, tell him that the Lord needs them, and he will send them right away." (Matthew 21:2-3, NIV)

If we find someone getting into our car, we would shout, "Hey, what are you doing, taking my car?" Yet here are two strangers doing precisely that, and the owner doesn't say a word because "the Lord needs them."

"I need no bullocks from your farms, no goat out of your herds... No, offer to God thanks as your sacrifice" (Psalm 50:9, 24, MOF)

Is this a contradiction? The donkey and colt, the Lord needs them, but "I have no need of a bull from your stall or goats from your pens, for every animal in the forest is mine and the cattle on a thousand hills." (Psalm 50:9-10, NIV) We cannot give the Lord anything that is not already His gift to us, but He delights in our offerings as an acknowledgement of His sovereignty. He does use us and our offerings to accomplish His purposes: "And Aaron shall offer the Levites before the Lord for an offering of the children of Israel, that they may execute the service of the Lord. (that they may be ready to do the work of the Lord)" (Numbers

8:11, KJV, NIV) "The Levites were consecrated to the service of the Lord in the place of the first-born: 'Sanctify unto me all the first-born, whatsoever openeth the womb among the children of Israel, both of man and beast: it is mine.'...I have taken the Levites from among the Israelites in place of the first male offspring of every Israelite woman. The Levites are mine." (Numbers 3:12, NIV) We saw in Chapter 1 how the Lord used our resources.

Accessing (1): Attitude

Most often we do not have the resources called for by the given situation. Our knowledge, our wealth, our influence etc. are most often woefully inadequate to the demands of the intercessory situation. Then why bother accessing our own resources? To acknowledge God as the source of every good and every perfect gift. "Everything comes from thee, and we only give thee what is thine." (1 Chronicles 29:14, NIV, MOF) Are there any loaves or fishes of mine that the Lord can use now?

Accessing (2): Identification

How real to us are the needs of the other persons? How would I act in the other person's circumstances? Where would I look for help? What are the loaves; what are the fishes that meet the need in the present instance?

Fortune 100 company executive

When told by an apprehensive senior executive of a Fortune 100 company that he was being reassigned from a line to a staff position, I tried to let him articulate how his 25-year experience could be put to much better use by the company. How would I help him by accessing my own resources? For him to articulate what vision he had for the company, he needed nuts-and-bolts knowledge of the corporation's past endeavors with potential parallels to the future endeavors.

As I prayed about it, I suddenly realized that in my research on integrating invention with innovation, I had studied his company. Later, he met me at my home where I shared the material I had developed in analyzing his company, which was new to him, and quite helpful in making his own case.

Accessing other Christians' experience – I

At the regular meeting of the Men's Ministry Committee, one member brought a sad and urgent matter for our intercession. The brother-in-law of an active Christian, "Gerry," whom we all knew, a young minister with three small children, had committed suicide. The minister was the brother of Gerry's wife, herself quite active in the large women's association of our church. What resources of mine could I access in behalf of Gerry?

As we went on with the business of the committee, I recalled someone I knew well in the church, from two summers earlier. "Johnson" also had faced the suicide of his wife's brother. I told the committee about it, and asked if anyone of the committee who was closer to Gerry would like to tell him about Jackson. At the chair's suggestion, I called "Johnson" myself and asked if he would talk to Gerry.

Accessing my own resources, in this instance, was accessing my memory of Johnson's experience of bearing the grief which the Lord could use as broken bread to strengthen Gerry. The next time I met Gerry, he said, "I received your message," referring to the message of concern and support I left on his answering machine. I asked him if Johnson called him. Gerry said yes, and gave the thumbs-up sign.

I know that I received a message of the Lord from what it does for the recipient. In this case, I knew from Gerry's beaming face and thumbs-up sign, that it was the Lord who asked me to ask Johnson to minister to Gerry, using his own suffering at his brother-in-law's suicide as the broken bread to nourish Gerry at his time of suffering.

Accessing other Christians' experience – II

After our committee meeting I was discussing with another member about interceding for Gerry the following week at our men's prayer breakfast. How would one claim a promise for Gerry? I recalled another suicide in a Christian family. In Taiwan, the missionary children go to a Christian school. Nurtured in isolation from the predominantly non-Christian environment for all their schooling, they face exceptional pressures when starting college in the States, to them a strange, almost foreign country.

One Tuesday morning, our devotions leader at our men's prayer breakfast sponsored by Taipei International Church, was called to the telephone. When he returned he told us that the son of one of the missionaries had committed suicide in the dormitory in the States. The young man was highly regarded during his school years in Taiwan, and apparently was doing well academically in the States.

Two weeks later, the father asked if he could preach the sermon at the Sunday morning worship service of Taipei International Church. He shared the anguish, the bewilderment, and the sense of helplessness that he and his family felt. When he returned from the States after the memorial service, he said that the wife of the senior missionary met him at the airport and said that the message she had received for him was, "When Jesus cried on the cross, 'My God, my God, why hast Thou forsaken me?' (Matthew 27:46, KJV) it answered all the questions of humanity on the problem of suffering."

His sermon text was "Master, carest thou not that we perish?" from

Jesus' stilling the storm. The preacher pointed out that Jesus was asleep; it looked as though he did not care what happened. The frantic disciples woke Jesus up. Jesus "rebuked the wind, and said unto the sea, 'Peace, be still.'" (Mark 4:39, KJV) And he chastised the disciples for their lack of faith. My recollection, many years later of the sermon message, is that when we feel abandoned by God as the disciples felt on the billowing sea, and as Jesus felt on the cross, we have to learn that even the wind and the sea obey him. (Mark 4:41, KJV)

Accessing (3): Awareness

To identify with the person's needs, we need to know them. We know them by listening actively. The very listening can make the person and us aware of nuances of the situation which may not have been clear before. Those nuances may help us make us aware of options not considered before. Are there other sources of help which the person can access?

Putting one's resources at the Lord's disposal

The Lord always asks for the resources that one has, not any resource that one does not have: "Have you caught anything, lads?" (John 21:5, PHI) No, they reply. Jesus tells them how to remedy their lack of fish: Cast the net on the right side of the boat. They catch 153 large fish. Then he says, "Bring some of the fish you've just caught." (John 21:10, PHI)

Again, in the feeding of the 5,000, Jesus asks the disciples for the resources they possess directly (none), or indirectly: How many loaves do you have? "He said, 'Bring them here to me.'" (Matthew 14: 18, MOF) The boy was willing to give up his entire lunch to Andrew, who would have told him, "The Lord hath need of them." (Matthew 21:3, KJV)

> KEY WORDS: Discerning The Lord's need; "Give ye them to eat"; attitude, identification

Discussion Starters – Chapter 14

1. Since we cannot possibly have the resources to meet all the needs of others that we intercede for, why bother accessing our resources at all?

2. "You Philippians will remember that in the early days of your acquaintance with the gospel when I set out from Macedonia, you were the only church who shared with me the fellowship of giving and receiving. Even in Thessalonica you sent me help when I was in need, not once but twice.... I am amply supplied, now that I have received from Epaphroditus the gifts you sent. They are a fragrant offering, an

acceptable sacrifice, pleasing to God." (Philippians 4:15-16,18, PHI, NIV) Discuss your church's missionary support. Do you write to them?

3. Share an instance in which you accessed your own resources for someone's concrete professional need.

4. Share an instance in which you accessed your own resources for someone's relational concrete need and spiritual concrete need.

5. What influences led to the boy sharing his whole lunch with Andrew who probably said that the Lord had need of it? Remember, he had no allowance he could spend to buy his lunch. Even if he had money, there were no fast food stores anywhere. He certainly could not have gone home to eat lunch. Would our children respond to a foreign missionary asking for such support?

6. Review 3 KEY WORDS: Discerning The Lord's need; "Give ye them to eat"; attitude, identification

Share a concrete need for which you accessed your own resources which was blessed manyfold for others.

15

LISCO (1): Listening To The Lord

The practice of prayer power is discussed under two acronyms DISCO (Chs. 12-14), and LISCO (Chs. 15-17). We do not rush in where we see a need, but await the guidance of the Spirit to discern the demand, claim a promise, and access our own resources. We listen to the Lord, communicate the message He gives us, and offer thanks for His provisions.

"Speak, LORD; thy servant is listening" (1 Samuel 3:9, KJV, MOF)

Samuel was about six years old. He did not know the Lord. "Now, in those days the word of the Lord was seldom heard, and no vision was granted." (1 Samuel 3:1, NEB) If there were no word from the Lord, it would be hard to recognize one when it came. That was Samuel's problem. He naturally assumed that the one who called him was his master, Eli, because "Samuel did not yet know the LORD: The word of the LORD had not yet been revealed to him." (1 Samuel 3:7, NIV) Eli instructed Samuel what to say the next time he was called; and he received a message from the Lord.

The highest gift

Imagine the privilege of being God's messengers – bringing to specific persons particular announcements that make the most sense only to them. It can be traumatic, as it was to Samuel: "Samuel feared to shew Eli the vision." (1 Samuel 3:15, KJV)For Ananias, being God's messenger (angel) was much more than traumatic. Carrying God's message to Saul who "still breathed threats of murder against the Lord's disciples," (Acts 9:1, MOF) was literally life-threatening to Ananias, who unlike Samuel, knew the Lord. So when the Lord called to him in a vision, "Ananias!" He answered, "Yes, Lord." (Acts 9:10, NIV) Samuel and Ananias were messengers of God – Angel Second Class: ASC. This job is very special, as we saw in chapter 1.

Listening: (1) Receiving and invoking scriptural promise

In chapter 12, we discussed "Claiming the promise." We start from the general promise as the ground of our claim, and ask the Lord to give us the specific promise to invoke to meet the particular concrete need.

From the general...

What right do we have to ask that the Lord of the universe stop in His tracks as it were, and attend to the single concrete need that is most pressing to me right now?

Because of the Lord's promise reinforced by the apostles' witness: "And I will do whatever you ask in my name, so that the Son may bring glory to the Father. You may ask me for anything in my name, and I will do it." (John 14:13-14, NIV) And the apostle's witness, "And my God will meet all your needs according to his glorious riches in Christ Jesus." (Philippians 4:19, NIV)

Note how unconditional the Lord's promise is: "whatever" and "anything." And Paul bears witness to God meeting all your needs, with no exceptions.

How can our concrete needs be met? By asking in His name. How do we ask in His name? By claiming a promise. When we ask the Lord to heal someone, to find a job for someone, we first pray that the Lord will show us what promise we should claim. When the Spirit gives us a promise to claim, it does not mean that the answer will be what we want. It will be what the Lord wants for us.

To the particular

Given the Lord's promise in the general – I will do whatever you ask in my name, we claim the promise in the particular: Lord, because you said something or did something, we ask Thee to meet a particular need of a particular person. Single sentence prayers with the first half the promise, and the second half the concrete need.

Listening: (2) Receiving and implementing a scriptural promise

Instead of an invoking promise to meet the need, we may be given a promise which implements (*implementing promise*) the fulfillment of need.

#35. Answered physical need: Facing a second miscarriage, Lisa receives promise – 1986-93 (expectant time)

At choir rehearsal on a Wednesday night in the Fall of 1986, we were told that Lisa, who had had one miscarriage, was starting to hemorrhage. I felt a call to pray for her. Toward the early hours on Thursday I suddenly woke up with a promise as her answer in the King James Version. I got up and searched for the verse using the concordance: "that your joy might be full." (John 15:11, KJV) Early Thursday, I contacted the choir director, but he did not have Lisa's number because she was new to the choir. I sought her out on Sunday and showed her the last phrases of the verse which were her promise.

Saying that we give promises in writing, I wrote the promise on the flyleaf of my *Interceding with the Infinite* book. She did give birth to Kelley in 1988 and Bryan in 1990. Before Bryan was born, she had to stay in bed for 10 weeks because of leakage. In January, 1993 she was once again ordered to stay in bed for the last 10 weeks of pregnancy. When I prayed for a promise to claim, I was told to ask Lisa to look up the written promise she already had. "So that is my promise?" she asked. I said, "Yes."

Listening Steps

How can we become angels when called upon by God to deliver messages? Through listening steps 1-4, the Four R's: Respond to the Lord – anytime, anywhere; Remember the word – chapter, verse, and version; Receive the invoking/implementing promise; and Reconfirm the invoking/implementing promise.

Listening Step 1: Respond to the Lord – anytime, anywhere

First and foremost, be available to the Lord when and where He needs you. Samuel was fast asleep when the Lord called him. Because he did not know yet the Lord, Samuel responded to Eli. Woken up from sleep, Samuel was ready and willing to do his master's bidding: "Here I am (Master Eli!)" (1 Samuel 3:4, NIV) As one who knew the Lord, Ananias answered when called, "Here I am, Lord." (Acts 9:10, NEB) So did Isaiah: "Here am I; send me." (Isaiah 6:8, MOF)

#36. Answered physical need: Daughter facing replacement of heart valve – 1985 (expectant time)

At a Tuesday prayer breakfast in Taipei, I spoke to Tom Diedricks, chairman of the Taipei International Church council and Leader of the prayer breakfast. He mentioned matter-of-factly that he and wife Mary would go to Seoul later in the week to pick up their daughter, Rebecca, a teacher at the Seoul International School. They would proceed to Mayo Clinic in Rochester, New York. To correct a congenital disorder, Rebecca's heart valve was replaced by a metal valve ten years earlier. The valve had now to be replaced with another in open-heart surgery.

I woke up around 3:15 A.M. with a strong sense of the ordeal that the Diedricks were facing – the sixteen-hour flight to New York, transfer to the Rochester flight. Most of all, I sensed the agony and uncertainty of the long hours of waiting that lay ahead for Tom and Mary when Rebecca would be prepared for surgery, operated on, and sent to recovery.

The unmistakable message for Tom and Mary that came to my mind was the two pillars that went before and after the children of Israel. Unless the message is specifically from one version or other, such as King James, I study different versions to develop a composite message from whichever versions as appropriate until I feel that the composite conveys precisely the message I received. NIV says, "By day the Lord went ahead of them in a pillar of cloud to guide them on their way and by night in a pillar of fire to give them light, so that they could travel by day or night." (Exodus 13:21, NIV) I typed up the message as I received it, and sent by prompt mail hoping that it would reach Tom and Mary before they left Taiwan.

I had no idea if Tom and Mary received my letter in time. But two years later, Tom said, "George, I haven't told you this. But you gave me a message at a very difficult time. When we were taking Rebecca for her open-heart surgery, all through the long hours, your letter told us that everything would be alright, and that encouraged us greatly. We knew it would be alright. Thanks."

Notice the time at which I was woken up: 3:15 A.M.! "But , Lord, do you know what time it is? Of course, He does. I am delighted that He saw fit to give His implementing promise through me to Tom and Mary, and that I responded to the Lord when He chose to call me. How do I know that the message was indeed from the Lord? By the results. Breaking through his conservative demeanor, Tom's gratefulness to the Lord came through when he said that through the long ordeal, he knew it would be alright. The message is for the recipient. And it spoke directly to Tom.

Listening Step 2: Remember the Word – chapter, verse, and version

If we don't know the Word, the Lord cannot give us an invoking/implementing promise from the Scripture wherein we have a carte blanche for all our needs:

> And I will do whatever you ask in my name, so that the Son may bring glory to the Father. You may ask me for anything in my name, and I will do it. (John 14:13-14, NIV)
>
> And my God will meet all your needs according to his glorious riches in Christ Jesus. (Philippians 4:19, NIV)

This is like a billion-dollar line-of-credit opened in your name: Pay to the order of you. It is drawn on the bank of Heaven, resources unlimited. Then why do we need to claim promises of the Lord for each concrete need as it arises? Because we have to write small checks for the grocery, for gas, and other concrete needs. Unlike our writing the individual checks drawing down our bank balances, the resources guaranteed by the Lord's carte blanche does not get used up. On the contrary, every check that we write – each promise that we claim In His Name – makes us active and fruitful in the knowledge of Jesus Christ.

Human sympathy and genuine well-wishing – Not God's promises

When faced with human distress, our hearts go out to them. We tell them: You will be alright; things will work out. We may wish with all our heart that our well-wishes will indeed come to pass. But they are not God's promises.

In chapter 6, we discussed #19. Answered professional need: Guilty verdict reversed in re-trial; Lost Job replaced. One fellow choir member went to "Jane" who had lost her job and was in the throes of a re-trial and facing the incompetence of her lawyer, and said, "It will be alright." She thanked him, but it was clear that she drew no strength to meet her burden from that well-wish, however sincere it was.

Three Scripture verses as answer to intercession:

We recall that Jane asked the soprano shepherd for intercession in her behalf, and three of us met to pray for her before choir practice.

As I prayed, two Scriptural references began to emerge. During the first half of the rehearsal, the messages came back, unbidden, in identical form. So, I wrote them out for Jane during the rehearsal break.

As we saw in chapter 6, the Scripture was fulfilled to the letter. That was the Lord's promise, and it demonstrated its unique power to meet the concrete need of Jane.

Lamp and light

Bound by our finiteness in time and space, we do not know how our concrete needs will be met. Each time the Lord lets us invoke a promise or gives us an implementing promise, He affirms us as part of that cloud of witnesses: "Wherefore seeing we also are compassed about with (surrounded by) so great a cloud of witnesses," (Hebrews 12:1, KJV, NIV) who act on the certainty that "all things work together for good to those who love God, those who have been called in terms of his purpose." (Romans 8:28, KJV, MOF) How could they be certain that it would be so? Because "Thy word is a lamp to guide my feet and a light for my path." (Psalm 119:105, NEB, NIV)

Furnishing faith with resolution

The lamp cannot guide or light the path unless it is lit. The Holy Spirit must light the lamp to guide us. But the Spirit has to speak to us in language we understand, so it is imperative that we know the Scripture. Peter urges us to "Make it your whole concern to furnish your faith with resolution." (2 Peter 1:5, MOF) Resolution is a resolute quality of mind, showing a fixed, firm purpose. Peter lists resolution as the first of seven qualities which "render you active and fruitful in the knowledge of our Lord Jesus Christ." (2 Peter 1:8, MOF)

Make it your whole concern to render you active and fruitful in the knowledge of our Lord Jesus Christ. The key to being active and fruitful is knowledge; "If ye abide in me, and my words abide in you, then ask whatever you wish and it will be given you. As you bear rich fruit and prove yourselves my disciples, my Father is glorified." (John 15:7-8, KJV, MOF, NIV) The knowledge is direct, intimate and unique, the very first Biblical reference underscoring these three characteristics being: "And Adam knew his wife." (Genesis 4:1, KJV) Peter is saying that we become active and fruitful when we know the Lord and His words directly, intimately, and uniquely. That knowledge must be our whole concern.

Writing in our hearts

The Word has to be ingrained in our very being. It is not our words that mediate God's grace, but what the Spirit does with our being to utter groanings that defy utterance. Identical Scripture will and must mean different outcomes depending on whom the Spirit uses to intercede. When the Word is written in our hearts, it will indeed be used by the Spirit to give us invoking and implementing promises."I will... write (my law) in their hearts...(and) they shall all know me." (Jeremiah 31:33-34, KJV, NIV)

Living meaning of the Word, and the Word giving meaning to living

Writing the Word in our hearts means knowing the letter of the Word, and more importantly, its meaning. To know the meaning, we must understand the context and content. That is why we have new translations of the Bible. Consider a familiar King James passage: "add to your faith virtue" (2 Peter 1:5). I do not know what "virtue" really means. When I look at New International Version, it says: "add to your faith goodness." Goodness is more understandable. But what is "add?"New English Bible gives a clue: "supplement your faith with virtue." Phillips says: "see that your faith carries with it real goodness of life."

How important is adding to your faith virtue? KJV says: "giving all diligence, add to your faith virtue." "Diligence" means perseverance, constant effort; make a constant effort to add virtue to faith. NIV says: "make every effort to add to your faith goodness." NEB is more helpful: "you should try your hardest to supplement your faith with virtue." Phillips is more descriptive: "you must do your utmost from your side, and see that your faith carries with it real goodness of life."

Peter cites seven characteristics beginning with virtue that must added to faith. Why? "They (these things) make you that ye shall neither be barren nor unfruitful in the knowledge of our Lord Jesus Christ." (2 Peter

1:8, KJV) It doesn't exactly make me want to rush out to add virtue to my faith.

NIV helps me understand what these "things" are: they are qualities: "They (these qualities) will keep you from being ineffective and unproductive in your knowledge of our Lord Jesus Christ." NEB gives a different slant on the qualities: they are gifts. "These are gifts which, if you possess and foster them, will keep you from being either useless or barren in the knowledge of our Lord Jesus Christ." Phillips also refers to "qualities": "If you have these qualities it means that knowing our Lord Jesus Christ has not made your lives either complacent or unproductive." Not exactly a rousing pep talk to rush out to see that your faith carries with it real goodness of life.

It was Moffatt's translation which suddenly made Peter's plea on the seven qualities spring to life. (1) It is not a question of diligence or even making every effort: "Make it your whole concern," says Moffatt's translation. Now that is far more demanding that diligence and even making every effort.

(2) What should I make it my whole concern? "Not adding to faith, virtue, but to furnish your faith with resolution." Resolution is a resolute quality of mind, showing a fixed, firm purpose. (3) Why should I make it my whole concern to furnish faith with resolution? "Because these qualities render you active and fruitful in the knowledge of our Lord Jesus Christ." The double negatives of neither be barren nor unfruitful are swept aside to the double positives of active and fruitful. In Moffatt's translation, Peter sweeps into rhetorical eloquence:

> Inasmuch as his power divine has bestowed upon us every requisite for life and godliness by the knowledge of him who called us to his own glory and excellence – bestowing on us thereby promises precious and supreme, that by means of them you may escape the corruption produced within the world by lust, and participate in the divine nature – for this very reason, do you contrive to make it your whole concern to furnish your faith with resolution, resolution with intelligence, intelligence with self-control, self-control with steadfastness, steadfastness with godliness, godliness with brotherliness, and brotherliness with Christ love. For as these qualities exist and increase with you, they render you active and fruitful in the knowledge of our Lord Jesus Christ. (2 Peter 1:3-8, MOF)

Promises precious and supreme to escape corruption by lust

What do the promises – precious and supreme – protect us from? From lust. What is lust? The dictionary meaning is "a desire to gratify the senses." (*Webster's New World Dictionary,* World, New York, 1970, p.844) Oswald Chambers defines lust in a somewhat unexpected manner: "Lust means – I must have it at once." (*op. cit.*, p. 38) Notice that he includes not only physical but also mental, emotional, and spiritual desires – all of them have one characteristic in common: now. We train ourselves from childhood on to defer gratification: not now. Chambers traces all dejection to lust:

> Dejection springs from one of two sources – I have either satisfied a lust or I have not. Lust means – I must have it at once. Spiritual lust makes me demand an answer from God, instead of seeking God Who gives the answer. What have I been trusting God would do? And today – the immediate present – is the third day, and He has not done it, therefore I imagine I am justified in being dejected and in blaming God. *(Ibid.)*

We can look upon lust as the prayer: My will be done-and right now – the opposite of what Jesus prayed in Gethsemene. When we ask the Spirit what promise we should claim for the particular situation, we are not placing an ultimatum on God, but acknowledging our finiteness and utter dependence on Him from everything, starting with the very breath we take. His promises sometimes lift the veil of time and give us a peek into the future as Abram, Elisabeth and Mary were privileged to do. But in seeking the Lord's promise for the particular need, we are acknowledging our dependence and finiteness, bowing to His infinite sovereignty.

Listening Step 3: Receive the invoking/implementing promise

How do you receive a promise from God? We will discuss my receiving two promises: an invoking promise to meet the recurring concrete needs of the choir members, and an implementing promise to meet a serious financial need for a man-of-Fourth (The men's group at Fourth Presbyterian Church).

#37. Answered spiritual need: Receiving message for the choir devotions – 1993 (expectant time)

One Sunday night, the phone rang. It was our choir devotions leader. She asked if I would take the devotions at the Wednesday choir rehearsal. I said I had kept back, letting others have their chance. She said, "Others have had their chance. When I prayed about devotions, your name came right up." As I listened to her, I tried to sense if the Lord wanted me to do the devotions. I told the her that since the Lord hadn't told me not to do the devotions, I would take it for Wednesday.

Right after she hung up, I prayed and asked the Lord what message He wanted me to give Wednesday. The words "resolution," "faith with resolution", "furnish faith with resolution" came to mind. After diligent searching, I could tell the choir that the message I received for us (the choir) was 2 Peter 1:5:

> The message I have been given for us tonight is 2 Peter 1:5 as it is found in Moffatt's translation, "Make it your whole concern to furnish your faith with resolution." (2 Peter 1:5, MOF) Resolution is a resolute quality of mind, showing a fixed, firm purpose. Peter lists resolution as the first of seven qualities that "render you active and fruitful in the knowledge of our Lord Jesus Christ." (2 Peter 1:8, MOF) "Render you active and fruitful." If I were to give a title to the devotions tonight, I would call it Making our Choir Active and Fruitful – spiritually, of course.
>
> I praise God for this choir because as a body, it praises and it prays. Could we become more active and fruitful in our prayer by claiming the power that is available to us in the Lord's promises: "*And I will do whatever you ask in my name,* so that the Son may bring glory to the Father. You may ask me for anything in my name, and I will do it." (emphasis added). (John 14:13-14, NIV) And the Apostle's witness: "And my God will *meet all your needs* according to his glorious riches in Christ Jesus." (emphasis added). (Philippians 4:19, NIV)
>
> How do we ask in His name? By claiming a promise. When we ask the Lord to heal someone, to find a job for someone, we first pray that the Lord will show us what promise we should claim. When the Spirit gives us a promise to claim, it does not mean that the answer will be what we want. It will be what the Lord wants in the circumstances.
>
> Here is an Intercession Request you can pick up during the cookie and juice break tonight. Mary wants us to put our filled requests in the basket on the piano. She will have them put together, and by Sunday find an Intercessor for next Wednesday. That intercessor will claim a promise for each need. Lord, because you said so , or did so, we ask Thee to meet such-and-such need of so-and-so. Single sentence prayers with the

first half the promise, and the second half the concrete need. My experience at Taipei International Church was that from the third week on we had Identified Answers for concrete needs.

#38. Answered financial need: Receiving a message for a Men-of-Fourth member in "serious financial condition" – 1993 (expectant time)

At the men's prayer breakfast, one of the prayer requests was for "Jake's" "serious financial condition." The following Wednesday, when I was shaving, I was seized of a strong feeling that Jake was in dire peril from a lion. It is as though a lion was about to attack him, and that I had to intercede then and there for him – which I did. The strong sense recurred two or three times in the next several minutes. Afterwards, I felt that the "lion's attack" was under control.

I wondered what the "lion's attack" was all about. Was Jake being called on the carpet by his boss; was he threatening to "fire" him? Whatever it was, after the repeated intercessions, the situation was under control.

The message is, of course, for the recipient. It is to him that it must speak. I left a message for Jake Thursday evening. He called back around 10 P.M. I asked him if anything special was happening during 8-9 A.M.? He couldn't recall anything out of the ordinary. I told him that I was asked to intercede for his situation. He said, "That is good news."

The serious financial condition was not at his work. It was a court case in which a motorist whose car he had bumped from behind several years earlier had filed a suit. Her payment demands far exceeded the limits of his insurance coverage. Did Jake have a lawyer? Yes. But the situation was being handled primarily by the lawyers of the insurance company. Jake had a lawyer, but the principal players were the insurance lawyers. "How does it look?" I asked. "Could go either way," he replied.

I went to bed after midnight. I was woken up at 3:17 A.M. on Friday with a strong sense that I should intercede for Jake's condition. I did. The "lion's attack" again came to mind. Was the reference to the lion which killed the prophet who disobeyed God? "As he went on his way, a lion met him on the road and killed him, and his body was thrown down on the road, with both the donkey and the lion standing beside it." (1 Kings 13:24, NIV) It did not appear so.

During the next hour and a half I mentally searched the Scripture for a message for Jake, asking the Lord if I should ask for an invoking or implementing promise. Different passages/events came to mind, but none were indicated as the applicable promise. The recurring theme was muzzling the mouth of the "lion", the restraints on a powerful attack. At 4:45 A.M. the promise came through unmistakably. I looked up the concordance and found the passage: "My God hath sent his angel, and hath shut the lions' mouths, that they have not hurt me." (Daniel 6:22, KJV)

I called him at 6:30 A.M. and said:" You know that the Lord woke me up at 3: 17 A.M. to intercede for you? He doesn't think I need any sleep! I have a message for you. You got a pencil? It is Daniel 6:22, the first half." Jake asked, "Something good?" "That is between you and the Lord. I just give you the message!" Saturday morning I saw "Jake." I asked him: Was (the message) alright?" "Yes," he said. "When is the settlement meeting?" He answered: in ten days.

Listening Step 4: Reconfirm the invoking/implementing promise

Recall that I apply Gideon's Rule to reconfirm the promise received whenever possible. A clear exception is in Ch. 5 (#15. Answered Physical Need: Precognition of one more year of life for a dying individual – 1982).

Prove me

Gideon, in his third and final test of his call to lead Israel against its enemies, uses the word "prove": "let me prove, I pray thee, but this once with the fleece; let it now be dry only upon the fleece, and upon all the ground let there be dew." (Judges 6:39, KJV) The word "prove" means "to find true." In a similar vein, Daniel wants to prove that abstaining from the king's meat and drink would not make the faces of Daniel and friends worse looking than those of their peers:

"Prove thy servants, I beseech thee ten days; and let them give us pulse to eat, and water to drink." (Daniel 1:12, KJV) In both instances, the action was counter-intuitive. It ran against reason to think that the fleece would be dry when there was dew upon the entire ground. Again it ran against reason that without the nutritious meat and wine from the king's table, Daniel and company would be "fairer and fatter." In both instances, counter-intuitive events prevailed.

Taste the Lord

NIV uses "test" where KJV uses "prove." The intent is "to find true" a statement that is so blatantly contrary to commonsense and convention. The Psalmist exclaims the joy of first-hand experience of the Lord as the best proof, the best test: "O taste and see that the Lord is good" (Psalm 34:8, KJV) Taste is a test.

While the fleece test was external to Gideon, the pulse diet test was internal to Daniel. Tasting is internal to the taster. It is intimate evidence. Only the person tasting sugar can say how sweet it is; the loud statements about the sweetness of sugar are put to flight by the child who says, "I tasted sugar; it is sweet." So also, as messengers, we have to taste the Lord to know Him. It is that tasting upon which depends our receiving and reconfirming the Lord's promises to meet concrete needs of ours and others.

KEY WORDS:Invoking promise; implementing promise; listening steps

Discussion Starters – Chapter 15

1. What is the "catch" in the unequivocal promise of the Lord: "And I will do whatever you ask in my name, so that the Son may bring glory to the Father. You may ask me for anything in my name, and I will do it." (John 14:13-14, NIV) "And my God will meet all your needs according to his glorious riches in Christ Jesus." (Philippians 4:19, NIV)

2. How do we know that we have met the condition in (1)?

3. What is the most inconvenient time when the Lord called you to do something for somebody else?

4. Share two instances in which you received the Lord's promise for concrete needs of (1) others, (2) you.

5. How did you reconfirm that the promises in (4) were indeed the Lord's?

6. Review KEY WORDS: Invoking Promise; Implementing promise; Listening Steps

Share an impulse to intercede that you obeyed which brought a blessing.

16

LISCO (2): Communicating The Message

The practice of prayer power is discussed under two acronyms DISCO (Chs. 12-14), and LISCO (Chs. 15-17). We do not rush in where we see a need, but await the guidance of the Spirit to discern the demand, claim a promise, and access our own resources. We listen to the Lord, communicate the message He gives us, and offer thanks for His provisions.

"Tell my servant David, thus saith the LORD" (2 Samuel 7:5, KJV)

In 1042 B.C. King David concludes over two decades of continuous fighting. the Lord had given him rest round about from all his enemies. (2 Samuel 7:1) Comparing the opulence of his own palace with the starkness of the house of the ark of God, David tells Nathan the prophet, "Here I live in a palace of cedar, while God's ark is inside the curtains of a tent!" (2 Samuel 7:2, NEB, NIV, MOF) Nathan says, "Go and do whatever is in your mind, for the Lord is with you." (2 Samuel 7:3, MOF, NEB) David's desire is most commendable: Build a beautiful temple.

"Go and give my servant David this message" (2 Samuel 7:5, MOF)

That night, the Lord tells Nathan what he should tell David. That message contradicts what Nathan told David earlier in the day. The well-meaning prophet, who approved David building the temple, must now reverse himself.

Nathan is given a lesson, like Peter, but much less severely. Good is the enemy of the best: "You think as men think, not as God thinks" ("Your outlook is not God's but man's") (Matthew 17:23, NEB, MOF) Nathan couldn't see any reason why David, whom the Lord called a man after His own heart, whom the the Lord had finally given peace, should not be encouraged to build the beautiful temple. Even Peter, who was commended by the Lord for his marvelous insight: "You are the Christ, the Son of the living God," (Matthew 16:16, NIV) could not see why the Lord could not be protected from the cross: "God bless you, Master! Nothing like this must happen to you!" (Matthew 16:22, PHI) This earned him the condemnation, "Get behind me, you Satan! (Matthew 16:23, MOF)

Both Nathan and Peter needed to be corrected because their outlook was not God's but man's. Moffatt's translation uses the word "message": "Go and give my servant David this message." That message may run completely counter to what we think the message ought to be. But the command is imperative: give this message.

"What did the Lord say to you? Do not hide it from me" (1 Samuel 3:17, NEB)

Whatever the message, the messenger must deliver it without fear or favor. Boy Samuel was "afraid to tell Eli about the vision." (1 Samuel 3:15, NEB) Who wouldn't be? Eli was the father figure whom Samuel knew all his short life from age two on. Then the Lord told him that his father's family was going to be dealt with severely. "See, I am about to do something in Israel that will make the ears of everyone who hears it tingle." (1 Samuel 3:11, NIV)

When the message to be conveyed is hard, as it was indeed in the case of Samuel, we may try to delay giving the message, or even try to soften it. But we have no business doing either. Let the Lord treat the recipient of the message as He will; He knows what is best for the recipient. We should never "interpret" the Lord's message. It is for the recipient to ask the Lord and receive the interpretation. Our job is to deliver it precisely as we received.

"You must go...Go at once to Straight Street" (Acts 9:15,11, NEB)

And the message may well reverse what we ourselves had told the recipient before we received the message, as Nathan did. When the Lord gives us a message for someone, that overrules everything prior, including our own sympathetic response to what seems a perfectly proper thing to do.

If anybody had a reason to delay, or even deny, the message to be transmitted, it was Ananias. He was, rightly, in mortal fear of "Saul still breathing threats of murder against the disciples of the Lord." (Acts 9:1, MOF, KJV) When the Lord told him to lay hands on Saul and restore his sight, Ananias says, "But, Lord, many people have told me about all the harm this man has done to thy saints in Jerusalem! And in this city too he has authority from the high priest to put anyone in chains who invokes thy Name!" (Acts 9:13-14, MOF, NEB)

Despite Ananias' genuine fear for his life, he is asked to do three things: (1) physical healing from blindness; (2) spiritual empowering by the gift of Holy Spirit; and (3) sacramental rebirth through baptism. Restoring sight to Saul might immediately put Ananias in chains, but the Lord wants the Jewish Christian to see in the renegade God's chosen instrument. The command is unequivocal: "But the Lord said to him, 'You must go, for this man is my chosen instrument to bring my name before the Gentiles and their kings as well as before the sons of Israel'" (Acts 9:15, NEB, MOF)

Communicating Steps

How can we become angels when called upon by God to deliver messages? Through Communicating Steps 1-4, the Four D's: Deliver the message without deviation; Deliver the message directly to the recipient; Dare to be held accountable; and Discover with the recipient the message.

Communicating Step 1: Deliver the message without deviation

First and foremost, deliver the message as given to you to deliver. Do not change an iota. If it is a verse of Scripture, be sure to communicate the chapter and verse and the version (KJV, Moffatt, NIV, NEB, Scoffield, etc.) Let the recipient himself read the Scripture, so that the Lord can tell him what the particular message is. Be sure neither to add nor subtract anything. Eli said to boy Samuel, "God kill you and worse, if you hide from me a single word of what (God) told you!" (1 Samuel 3:17, MOF)

Communicating Step 2: Deliver the message directly to the recipient

The best form of delivery is face-to-face with the intended recipient. Where that is not possible, be sure to give the message in writing. When I communicate a verse using different translations, I type the message precisely as it is given to me. The particular way the different versions are spliced together is fundamental to the message. For instance, the message is totally different when it is "Furnish your faith with Resolution" (Moffatt), and not "Add to your faith virtue." (KJV), although the verse is identical: 2 Peter 1:5. If the Lord uses different versions, use them to communicate the message precisely, and not approximately.

From experience I have found that when I have had to communicate a message through a third party, the result has never been satisfactory. Despite the best intentions, the third party can never tell the message the way you can.

Communicating Step 3: Dare to be held accountable

Who says something is equally, if not more, important than what he says, "Look, in this town there is a man of God; he is highly respected, and *everything he says comes true*. Let's go there now. Perhaps he will tell us what way to take. " (emphasis added). (1 Samuel 9:6, NIV)

Why should one listen to the man of God? Because of his track record. "You may say to yourselves, 'How can we know when a message has not been spoken by the Lord?' If what a prophet proclaims in the name of the Lord does not take place or come true, that is a message the Lord has not spoken. That prophet has spoken presumptuously. Do not be afraid of him." (Deuteronomy 18:21-22, NIV)

When Samuel was 59, he had a long track record which Saul's servant referred to in suggesting that they seek God's guidance on their errand of locating missing donkeys through prophet (seer) Samuel. In fact, Samuel was acknowledged as a prophet at age 6 when he gave Eli the prophecy regarding the house of Eli. "As Samuel grew up, the Lord was with him, and none of his words went unfulfilled. From Dan to Beersheba, all Israel recognized that Samuel was confirmed as a prophet of the Lord." (1 Samuel 3:19-20, NEB)

But only a Samuel can bat a thousand. Consider prophet Nathan. He told David, "Go and do whatever is in your mind, for the Lord is with you." Surely, David had no reason to doubt that Nathan was speaking God's message. But God gives Nathan a counter-intuitive message. And Nathan goes to David and tells him the Lord's message without any deviation.

As Angels Second Class (ASC), we deliver the Lord's messages. Can we err? Certainly. Even Nathan did. How can we reduce the chance of error? Gideon's Rule is one method, but even that is not foolproof. While to the best of our conscious knowledge, the message is repeated unbidden three or more times, there could be deep-seated sympathies of ours which may have influenced the recall.

All we can do is to tell the recipient how we have received the message, and how we have tried to be truly open to the Lord for His message. With that caveat, we Dare to be held accountable. The test is: Does the message speak to the recipient in his situation?

Communicating Step 4: Discover with the recipient the message

Ask the recipient, "What does the message mean to you?" Be prepared for the message to be totally different from what you expected it to be. By following up with the recipient on what he experienced as the meaning, we learn that the Lord meets our needs abundantly in ways totally unexpected. We will discuss three instances which illustrate the poverty of my imagination.

#39. Answered professional need: Receiving a message for "Joan" in desperate need – 1985 (expectant time)

In chapter 8, #24. Answered professional need recounted how "Joan," who was unemployed for 913 days found "dream job" in 23 days. The next year, Joan found out that the "Dream Job" was soon going to end.

It will be recalled that a career-oriented resumé that I prepared for Joan was very helpful, even though resumé-writing was not my profession.

As she spoke on the phone, quite early one morning, about her need for a new job, I remember being half-asleep, but nevertheless receiving the picture of the disciples going back to fishing after the resurrection, but their catching nothing all night until Jesus told them to change their direction. I recalled the incident to Joan. She remembered. I said, "Remember Jesus said to the disciples: Cast the net on the right side of the ship." (John 21:6, KJV) In fact, I recalled it as cast the net on the other side of the ship.

As messenger, I do not interpret the message; that is between the Lord and the recipient. Yet, as an interested observer, I wondered what the "other side" meant. Since Joan had found that the new resume I wrote for her was instrumental in in finding her "dream job", and several questions that the prospective employer put to Joan were couched in the very words of the resumé, I thought that perhaps Joan's skills had to repackaged with a different focus. Of course, I did not share my reasoning with Joan.

It was a good thing that I didn't. The message Joan received was entirely different. What does the "other side" mean? I asked. Without hesitation, she said, "I am ready for a change. I should go to California," she said. It sounded somewhat preposterous to talk of California when she couldn't find a job in Washington, where she had lived and worked for several years. Miraculously, she left for California within two months for an excellent managerial position in an industry she had never worked in!

#40. Answered professional need: Receiving a message for Jake – 1992 (expectant time)

In Chapter 15, #38. Answered financial need related to Jake receiving a reassuring message when facing a serious financial condition.

A year earlier, Jake gave his testimony at the men's retreat. With a family to support, his inadequate income and benefits were most anxiety-provoking. During the thirteen months of search for a new job, Jake continued to tithe. There were times when they did not know where the next meal would come from. And there were bags of grocery left outside the door by anonymous donors from the church just in time for the next meal. Each month they would look at the bills for their family with small children, and wonder how they would be met. But the Lord was faithful, and each month there was enough money to meet all the bills and pay the tithe. He thanked the many good Christians who reached out to him with gifts of money and food. "What I need is a good job!" he said.

When I was led to intercede for Jake, the repeated message coming to mind was the first fish that Peter caught which contained the precise amount of the poll tax: "Go to the lake and throw out your line. Take the first fish you catch; open its mouth and you will find a four-drachma coin. Take it and give it to them for my tax and yours." (Matthew 17:27, NIV) I communicated to Jake the message. Could it mean a made-to-order job for Jake?

Several days later, I asked Jake what the message meant to him. He said that he and his wife tried to find the meaning for him of the message. It did not seem to point to a new job. Since the Biblical reference was to tax, could it point to something in tax – such as tax refund? It was; they had a tax refund coming to them!

#35. (Conclusion) Answered physical need: Promise received, but miscarriage not avoided – 1986-93 (expectant time)

In Chapter 15, we discussed Lisa facing a second miscarriage, receiving the message, "that your joy might be full." (John 15:11, KJV) As a messenger, I communicate no more and no less than what I am given; the recipient should receive from the Lord His message. My wife was concerned that we might interpret the promise to mean that the miscarriage would be avoided. Given the heartbreak of the first miscarriage, it is perfectly understandable if Lisa interpreted the promise to mean that her joy might be full by becoming a family. I very much wished for her to carry the baby to term. But she miscarried a second time.

As we saw in the last chapter, after the second miscarriage, she was blessed with three healthy births. The promise was: That your joy might be full. Did it mean forming a family? Did it mean immediately? Finite humans that we are, especially Americans, we look for instant gratification. But the promise did not specify instant gratification of our need. It was filled far more abundantly – later – in His time.

We also saw in the last chapter that Lisa was ordered to bed rest for ten weeks prior to her third delivery in 1993. She announced to the choir the doctor's suspicion that the leakage was the amniotic fluid. If so, he would order her to bed rest until delivery. To Lisa, bed rest was not something she wished for. "Last time when I had to do it, I had communion with the Lord, but it was most miserable to be on your back all the time. It is worse this time with two babies to take care of by myself. (Husband) James leaves for work at 5:30 in the morning. His office changed the insurance carriers, and I won't have a helper for the babies as I did last time. Please pray that I won't have to go through ten weeks of bed rest again!"

I asked for a promise – invoking or implementing promise. As I said in the last chapter, the message was: Ask her to read the promise. The reference was what I wrote down for her in 1986 – something I no longer remembered in 1993. She looked it up. I asked, "What does that tell you?"

At the Wednesday choir rehearsals we would hear from neighbor Pat that Lisa was most depressed. At the second report, we were encouraged to sign up to provide food, baby care and housework. And the response was immediate and gratifying. "We have never been fed so well," declared Lisa. "Everyone has been so nice and caring." She found a new meaning to the message: the joy of knowing the love of the choir family.

KEY WORDS: Dare to be held Accountable;"Give this message"; Communicating Steps

Discussion Starters – Chapter 16

1. How do you know that you have a message from the Lord for someone?

2. Discuss a message which, on the face of it, appeared irrelevant, but when you communicated, became the precise promise for the need.

3. "Look, in this town there is a man of God; he is highly respected, and everything he says comes true. Let's go there now. Perhaps he will tell us what way to take. " (1 Samuel 9:6, NIV)

Recall the very first message that you communicated. How did you feel about the trust the recipient was placing in you as ASC?

4. Recount how you misinterpreted a message, but the Lord taught you through your (and the recipient's) reading your hopes into the promise.

5. "If only you had been here, Lord," said Martha, "my brother would never have died, And I know that , even now, God will give you whatever you ask from him." (John 11: 21-22, PHI) You have prayed for someone critically ill. You have received a message. How do you help the recipient to open his heart to understand the message?

6. Review KEY WORDS: Dare to be held accountable; "Give this message"; Communicating Steps
Share an instance in which you misinterpreted the Lord's message.

17

LISCO (3): Offering Thanks

The practice of prayer power is discussed under two acronyms DISCO (Chs. 12-14), and LISCO (Chs. 15-17). We do not rush in where we see a need, but await the guidance of the Spirit to discern the demand, claim a promise, and access our own resources. We listen to the Lord, communicate the message He gives us, and offer thanks for His provisions.

"Father, I thank you that you have heard me. I know that you always hear me." (John 11:41-42, PHI)

When Jesus purposely arrives late in Bethany, Lazarus has been dead for four days. While Jesus loved Martha and her sister (Mary) and (their brother) Lazarus, (John 11:4, NIV) NEB alone explains why he arrived late. "This illness will not end in death: it has come for the glory of God, to bring glory to the Son of God. And therefore, though he loved Martha and her sister and Lazarus, after hearing of his illness Jesus waited for two days in the place where he was." (John 11:4-6) Mary would later anoint Jesus' head and feet with an alabaster flask of expensive perfume, the extravagant outpouring of her love, receiving Jesus' commendation, "I tell you the truth, wherever the gospel is preached throughout the world, what she has done will also be told, as her memorial to me." (Matthew 26:13, NIV, PHI) Phillips uses present perfect as a preamble to prayer. "You have heard me; and it is a permanent prefix: You always hear me."

Thanksgiving Steps

When called upon by God to deliver messages, the 3 R's: offer thanks for the Resources given for needs; offer thanks for Relationship with the Lord; offer thanks Relinquishing the rare resources, reminding us to be thankful.

Thanksgiving Step 1: Offer thanks for the Resources given for needs

Jesus asks for Lazarus' life: "Lazarus, come out!" (John 11:43, MOF) What is the limit upon the resources that we may ask for? None at all! No limits are set in the Lord's promises. "And I will do whatever you ask in my name, so that the Son may bring glory to the Father. You may ask me for anything in my name, and I will do it" (John 14: 13-14, NIV)

Our thanks which we prefix to the prayer must therefore be for all the resources provided to abundantly meet our needs. "Bless the Lord, O my soul, and forget not all his benefits." (Psalm 103:2, KJV) Moffatt uses "remember" for "forget not." To actively remember God's benefits, we could count them. In Fig 3.1 we classified the resources in terms of their results:

> Result of newly-provided resources: Acceptance of Christ, spiritual growth, spiritual maturity, spiritual joy, ability to forgive, Other
> Dramatic physical healing, physical healing, remission of illness, ability to live with disease, ability to grieve, Other
> Receiving of funds (means of funds), obtaining of career placement, obtaining career advancement, receiving professional skills, Other
> Initiation of communications, initiation of broken communications, restoration of relationships, ability to live with hard relationships, Other.

We tend to overlook the most important resources: every breath we take; the gift of sight, sound, taste, smell; the gift of health; the gift of family and of friends; the gift of sunrise and sunset, snow and rain, summer and spring; the gift of grass and flowers, birds and bees, and so on. We should take time to acknowledge often the uncounted blessings which are ours.

Thanksgiving Step 2: Offer thanks for the Relationship with the Lord

The resources that the Lord provides are the symbol of the relationship we have with the Lord. The children of Israel had to learn again and again to focus not on the gifts, but the Giver.

A symbol of this relationship is seen in Jesus' prayer. We noted in chapter 1 three recorded occasions when Jesus looked up to heaven: (1) when he had taken the five loaves and the two fishes (2) the healing the deaf and near-mute, and (3) the farewell discourses in the Upper Room. At the tomb of Lazarus, the prologue to prayer is again an upward look. "And Jesus lifted up his eyes, and said Father, I thank thee that thou hast heard me." (John 11:41, KJV) Looking toward heaven or spreading one's hands toward heaven is to both affirm God's power and to invoke His providence: *divine dependence.*

We see Moses and Solomon practicing it. The Pharaoh asked Moses to beseech the Lord to stop the plague of thunder and hail: "And Moses went out of the city from Pharaoh, and spread abroad his hands unto the Lord: and the thunders and hail ceased, and the rain was not poured upon the earth." (Exodus 9:33, KJV) At the dedication of the temple, "Solomon stood before the altar of the Lord in the presence of all the congregation of Israel, and spread forth his hands toward heaven." (1 Kings 8:22, KJV)

As divine dependence becomes a reflex – an involuntary activity which occurs automatically without conscious deliberation – we feel the Lord's abiding presence and provision. We see this realization in the Psalmist who stands in utter awe at the thoughts of God toward him: "How precious to me are your thoughts unto me, O God! How inexhaustible their themes! Were I to count them, they would outnumber the grains of sand; to finish the count, my years must equal thine." (Psalm 139: 17-18, NIV, NEB, KJV) As parents we know how often we think of our children; the baby is always in the mother's thoughts. "Can a woman forget the infant at her breast, or a loving mother the child of her womb? Yet even were a mother to forget, never will I forget you." (Isaiah 49:15, NEB, MOF) The more real the relationship of the Lord with us, the closer our intercession becomes present perfect ("You have heard me"), instead of present plea ("Hear me when I call to you, O my righteous God" (Psalm 4:1, KJV, NIV))

Thanksgiving Step 3: Offer thanks Relinquishing the rare resources

Sometimes we are overwhelmed by the resources that are showered upon us by God.Do we pour it out unto the Lord as David did?

David was hiding in the cave of Adullam, with Philistines encamped in the Valley of Rephaim nearby. His three top heroes fought their way through the Philistines lines, because David said longingly, "Oh if someone would only give me a drink of water from the well at Bethlehem, the well beside the gate!" (2 Samuel 23:15, MOF) We should note that the three heroes had to fight through an army of Philistines around Jerusalem to get to the well, draw the water, and fight through another army (the Philistines encamped in the Valley of Rephaim) to bring the water to David. "But David refused to drink it; he poured it out to the Lord and said, 'God forbid that I should do such a thing! Can I drink the blood of these men who risked their lives for it?' So he would not drink it" (2 Samuel 23:16-17, NEB) We would hardly ever ask our closest friends to lay their lives on the line to satisfy some longing of ours. Oswald Chambers interprets it for us:

> What has been like water from the well of Bethlehem to you recently – love, friendship, spiritual blessing? Then at the peril of your soul, you take it to satisfy yourself. If you do, you cannot pour it out before the

> Lord. You can never sanctify to God that which you long to satisfy yourself...
> How am I to pour out unto the Lord natural love or spiritual blessing? In one way only – in the determination of my mind. There are certain acts of other people which one could never accept if one did not know God, because it is not within human power to repay them. But immediately I say – This is too great and worthy for me, it is not meant for a human being at all, I must pour it out unto the Lord, then these things pour out in rivers of living water all around. (*op. cit.*, p. 247)

KEY WORDS: All your needs; divine dependence; pouring out unto the Lord

Discussion Starters – Chapter 17

1. What is the ratio of praise to petition in your groups' prayer requests?

2. How are you encouraging yourself and others to be thankful to the Lord?

3. "And one of them finding himself cured, turned back, and with a loud voice glorified God; he fell on his face at the feet of Jesus and thanked him. The man was a Samaritan. And Jesus answering said, Were there not ten cleansed? But where are the nine? Could none be found to come back and give praise to God except this foreigner?" (Luke 17:15-18, KJV, NEB, MOF) Recount an experience in which you praised or helped praise God for meeting a special concrete need.

4. Has your own personal experience grown from results to relationship?

5. When he had taken the five loaves and the two fishes, he looked up to heaven. Recall an instance in which when faced with a difficult situation you instinctively looked up to heaven.

6. Compare DEAVECO with DISCO and LISCO together. What additional elements are covered by the latter?

101. Review KEY WORDS: All your needs; divine dependence; pouring out unto the Lord.

Share an instance of thanksgiving considered extravagant by others.

Answered prayers by concrete need

Financial

Need **Page**

#9. Seminary student meeting his tuition deadline – 1955 26
#11. Peter's first fish providing 65 cents for temple tax – A.D. 32 .30
#38. Someone in "serious financial condition" – 1993 124

Physical

#2. Recovery of teenager found motionless in pool—1993 4
#3. God Curing a king – B.C. 1807 19
#6. God giving Abram a son – B.C. 1897 24
#7 Christ restoring to life the Royal Official's son – A.D. 30 24
#8. Christ healing the centurion's servant – A.D. 31 25
#10. Kiwanian being rescued from upended car – 1990 27
#12 Elijah being fed twice daily for two years – B.C. 929 33
#13 Elijah being fed at home for a year and a half – B.C. 927 34
#15 Precognition of one more year of life – 1982 45
#16 Precognition of bedridden cancer patient's travel – 1983 45
#21 Prayer support of unspecified need 30 miles away – 1984 . .60
#23 One-and-a-half year old's right tear duct unblocked – 1984 .64
#26 Recovery from the point of death – 1991 72
#27 Large cyst disappearing before surgery – 1996 73
#35 Promise for one facing a second miscarriage – 1986-93 116
#36 Daughter facing replacement of heart valve – 1985 117

Professional

#1. Finding a new high-salary job – 1993 2
#18. Hostile superior blocking promotion reversed– 1986 50
#19. Guilty verdict reversed in retrial; lost job replaced– 1986 . . .53
#24. Professional unemployed for 913 days– 1994 65
#29. Regional manager abruptly out of a job– 1996 75
#30 Utterly frustrated professional – 1997 .77
#31 Dream delayed for seven years – 1953 83
#32 Professional contribution delayed – 1992 86
#39 A message for "Joan" in desparate need – 1985 131
#40 A message for "Jake" – 1992 131

Relational

#20 Prayer support provided from a half a world away – 1987 . . 59
#25 Initiation of broken communications – 1984 69
#28 Financial catastrophe of engaged couple reversed – 1996 . . . 74

Spiritual

#4 Christ restoring Peter – A.D. 33 20
#5 Saul becoming Paul – A.D. 34 20
#14 Precognition of one's own death – 1974; 1977 39
#17 Bright-raimented Robinson conveying his passage – 1985 . . 46
#22 Prayer support from US of need in Taipei – 1985 60
#33 Surrendering my right to define my profession – 1943 89
#34 Surrendering my right to a passport – 1953 90
#37 Receiving message for choir devotions – 1993 119

About the author

GEORGE KUTTICKAL CHACKO was born into a Mar Thoma Syrian Church family, believed to have been Christian since the year 52 when, tradition has it, four Hindu Brahmin families were converted to Christianity by the preaching of Thomas, the doubting disciple of Jesus Christ, in Kerala, India. He translated the ancient liturgy of his church and the order of holy matrimony into English.

Professor of Systems Science with the University of Southern California, 1970-94; Emeritus, 1974, he joined Universitit Pertanian Malaysia (near Kualalumpur) as Professor of Management in July, 1996 He is Malaysian Airlines System Professor of Technology Management and Chairman of the Joint MIT-UPM program in Management of Technology.

Author, editor, and / or contributor of 48 books in fields ranging from Operations Research and Management Science, computers and artificial intelligence to technology management and technology transfer, systems analysis and statistics, Dr. Chacko's biography appears in 15 references, including *Who's Who In America, Who's Who In The World,* and *Who's Who In Science and Engineering* (Premier Edition). His publications include: *Life Abundant Day by Day* and *Interceding with the Infinite.*

At Taipei International Church, he has served as Sunday School Superintendent, and been a member of the governing body chairing the committees of Worship, Membership, and Stewardship. At his home church, Fourth Presbyterian Church in Bethesda, Maryland, he is Founder-Director of Prayer Power Partnership, serves on the Men's Ministry Committee, sings in the Sanctuary Choir and edited *Lenten Daily Devotions, 1996.*